Winning TOEFL

Yuri Yi

Listening Step 2

Step 1

Step 2

Step 3

Winning TOEFL Listening Step 2

Copyright © 2009 by Yuri Yi

All rights reserved. No part of this publication may be reproduced, stored in a retrieval system, or transmitted, in any form, or by any means, electronic, mechanical, photocopying, recording or otherwise, without the prior written permission of the copyright holder and the publisher.

Published by PAGODA Books
PAGODA Books is the professional language publishing company of the PAGODA Education Group.
19F, PAGODA Tower, 419, Gangnam-daero,
Seocho-gu, Seoul, 06614, Rep. of KOREA
www.pagodabook.com

First published 2009
Sixteenth impression 2024
Printed in the Republic of Korea

ISBN 978-89-6281-061-5 (13740)

Publisher | Kyung-Sil Park
Writer | Yuri Yi

A defective book may be exchanged at the store where you purchased it.

Winning TOEFL

Listening Step 2

Introduction to iBT TOEFL

iBT TOEFL (internet-based TOEFL) is designed to measure how well non-native speakers of English read, listen, speak, and write in English. The test has four sections: reading, listening, speaking, and writing. Each section of the test is worth 30 points and the highest possible score on the iBT is 120 points (30 points x 4 sections). Most questions are worth 1 point each, but some of the questions in each section are worth more than 2 points.

 → For more information, visit the ETS website (www.ets.org).

Listening Section

(1) About the listening material

In the listening section, test takers are asked to listen to 4 or 6 lectures and 2 or 3 conversations. The length of each material varies from 500 to 800 in words, or 3 to 5 minutes in listening time.

Number of Passages	Types of Material	Test Time
6	4 Lectures 2 Conversations	60 min
9	6 Lectures 3 Conversations	90 min

There are two major types of listening material covering a wide range of topics that students need to listen in academic environment:
- Lectures: a talk given by a professor or a discussion with students on an academic subject in the classroom setting
- Conversations: a student talking to a professor, teaching assistant, school staff or employee about a situation related to student life

All material is recorded in natural spoken English from North America and other English-speaking parts of the world.

(2) About the questions

After listening to each material, several questions follow to test the ability of the test takers in the following areas:
- Basic Comprehension: ability to understand the main topic and idea of the material and detail information

- Pragmatic Understanding: ability to understand the function of what is said and recognize the speaker's attitude
- Connecting Information: ability to understand organization of the material, connect content and make inferences

In order to test these areas, there are six major types of questions asked in the iBT TOEFL listening section.

Question Type	Explanation	Related Unit
Basic Comprehension		
Main topic / idea	Asks about the overall topic or the central idea of the material	Unit 1
Supporting / Specific Details	Asks about specific information that are important points within the material	Unit 2
Connecting Information		
Organization	Asks about the overall structure and flow of the material	Unit 3
Content	Asks about the relationship and reasoning of specific information within the material	Unit 4
Pragmatic Understanding		
Function	Asks about the purpose or meaning of specific information or phrases	Unit 5
Stance and Attitude	Asks about the attitude or implied meanings of the speaker	Unit 6

Winning TOEFL Listening series**

This is the second listening book in *Winning TOEFL* series. It has 6 units, and each unit includes 6 lectures and 3 conversations in various lengths. This second book is designed for students who are beginners in academic listening. Therefore, the level of difficulty and the length of the listening material have been modified from the original materials seen on the actual TOEFL.

Each unit of this book deals with a specific academic topic and situation that appear frequently on the TOEFL:

	LECTURE TOPICS	CONVERSATION TOPICS
Unit 1	Natural Science	Class activities and registration
Unit 2	History	School admission
Unit 3	Applied Science	Student housings
Unit 4	Education and Language	Student jobs
Unit 5	Nature and Society	Student activities
Unit 6	Arts and Culture	School policies and facilities

Each unit consists of:

Introduction ➔ Practices I, II ➔ Tests 1, 2, 3 ➔ Listening Helper

Each section has the following subsections.

Introduction

(1) Key Expressions

Key Expressions are provided to help students become familiar with frequently used expressions in academic settings. Each unit carries different set of expressions that may be used with specific intentions. Students should pay attention to these expressions as signals for more important information while they are listening.

(2) Target iBT TOEFL Questions

This part is to prepare students with frequently asked question types in the iBT TOEFL listening test. Students are encouraged to listen for type of information that is more likely to appear in the questions. Each unit focuses on the following iBT TOEFL question types:

WINNING TOEFL LISTENING

Unit 1	Main idea and Topic Questions
Unit 2	Specific Detail Questions
Unit 3	Organization Questions
Unit 4	Content Questions
Unit 5	Function Questions
Unit 6	Attitude Questions

Practice 1, 2

The main purpose of this section is to lead students to listen to short passages (170 words in average) and find answers for target questions. Additional exercises with specific tasks follow to strengthen student's skills for keyword listening and summarization.

(1) Warm Up
This part is provided as a pre-listening exercise. Students are asked to choose one of the words inside the bracket to complete each sentence. (reflecting the topic of the following listening material) The purpose of this exercise is to familiarize students with the content of the lectures or discussions in the practice section.

(2) Part I: Practice 1, 2, 3 - With dictation exercises
In this part, students are asked to answer one target question for each listening material. Then the following dictation exercise asks students to listen again to fill in the blanks in the script provided. This exercise is designed to help students practice listening skills on linking sounds and sound confusions.

(3) Part II: Practice 4, 5, 6 - With summary exercises
In this part, students are asked to answer 2-3 questions including target questions for each listening material. Then the following summary exercise asks students to listen again to complete the summary notes. This exercise is designed to lead students to understand the overall flow of the material and be able to extract its key information.

(4) Vocabulary
Each practice question is provided with the list of key vocabulary. This list can be studied before students listen to the material in order to enhance students' understanding. It can also be reviewed afterward in the Listening Helper section.

Tests 1, 2, 3
In this section, students are required to listen to longer material (240 words in average) and answer 3-5 questions including each unit's target questions. This section is an opportunity for students to apply their skills acquired from the unit into more intensive practice.

Listening Helper
This part is provided to help students review and strengthen their knowledge of essential vocabulary. Students are asked to read or listen to each statement and complete it with the correct vocabulary. Each statement and the vocabulary have been taken from the practice section.

Actual Test
At the end of all 6 units, one set of actual test is provided. In this section, there are 6 listening materials (4 academic lectures and 2 conversations) followed by 3-5 questions. Although the lengths and the difficulty of the material have been modified to meet beginner's level, students are encouraged to take this section as an actual test taking opportunity.

Contents

Unit 1 Academic Lectures : Natural Science
         Conversations   010

Unit 2 Academic Lectures : History
         Conversations   028

Unit 3 Academic Lectures : Applied Science
         Conversations   046

Unit 4 Academic Lectures : Education and Language
         Conversations   064

Unit 5 Academic Lectures : Nature and Society
         Conversations   082

Unit 6 Academic Lectures : Arts and Culture
         Conversations   100

- **Actual Test**   118
- **Script & Answer Keys**

UNIT 01

Academic Lectures: Natural Science Conversations

•• Key Expressions

The speaker may use certain expressions as a signal to talk about the main topic or idea of the lecture.

- What I'd like to discuss now is…
- Let's look more closely at…
- I want to explain…
- Today, we're going to examine…

- Are you familiar with…?
- Do you know…?
- The interesting thing is…
- I'd like to begin by discussing…

•• Target iBT TOEFL Questions

Academic lectures

What is the main topic of the lecture/discussion?
What does the speaker mainly discuss?
What is the main idea of the lecture?

Conversations

What is the conversation mainly about?
What are the speakers mainly discussing?
Why does the student go to the registrar's office?

Practices

Warm Up 🔊 01_U1_WU.mp3

First, circle one of the words inside the bracket to complete each sentence with your own choice. Then listen to the recording to check the correct answer.

1. Flowers completed most of their evolutionary process in (30 / 13) million years.

2. Cats can see the world only in shades of (blue and yellow / black and white).

3. When we are hungry, thinking about food sends signals to our (brain / digestive organs).

4. Corn plants in the field often get invaded by (caterpillars / wasps).

Part I

Practice 1  02_U1_P1.mp3

A Listen to part of a talk given in a biology class. Pay attention to the main topic or idea and answer the question.

Q. What is the main idea of the lecture?

Ⓐ The evolution of flowers is completely unknown.
Ⓑ Flowers evolved in quite a short period of time.
Ⓒ Among scientists, biologists work the fastest.
Ⓓ Flowering plants actually appeared 30 million years ago.

B Listen again and fill in the blanks.

> **Prof(W):** Scientists say flowers first _____ on Earth about 140 million years ago. Then, by about 30 million years later, flowers completed _____ their evolutionary processes. Well, the interesting thing is that to a biologist, 30 million years of time is _____, so the evolutionary process of flowers is _____ to be very fast. That's why a group of scientists are now trying to solve the mystery _____ flowers' fast evolution. _____ to solve this mystery is to make a full _____ of a plant called 'Amborella.' The Amborella is a very important plant for the scientists because it is the _____ flowering plant. And now, many scientists hope that it can provide _____ clues about flowers' _____ and evolution.

• evolutionary	**adj** of the history of the development of a biological group
• genetic map	a graphic representation of the structure of a single genes
• flowering plant	a plant that produces flowers and fruit

 **Practice 2** 03_U1_P2.mp3

A **Listen to part of a lecture in a science class. Pay attention to the main topic or idea and answer the question.**

Q. What is the main topic of the lecture?

Ⓐ Ambushing predators
Ⓑ Detecting a cat's movement
Ⓒ Colorblind animals
Ⓓ Cats' vision

B **Listen again and fill in the blanks.**

Prof(M): Now, let's turn our attention to how cats _____. Some people consider cats to be _____. It is because cats see the world in _____ of blue and yellow, much _____ people who are red-green colorblind, so maybe cats' color vision isn't _____ as humans. However, cats' vision has _____ to detect movement. Have you seen a cat pounce when _____ moves? Then you've probably also _____ that it doesn't move when the toy _____ still. That's because cats are ambush predators. This means that cats _____ still and _____ moving prey. That's how ambush predators _____ their prey. Also, the position of the cat's eyes, _____ on the front of the head, makes the cat _____ judging distance.

• colorblind	**adj** being partly or totally unable to recognize one or more colors
• shade	**n** the gradation of darkness
• evolve	**v** to develop or achieve gradually
• detect	**v** to discover the existence or presence of a thing
• pounce	**v** to make a sudden approach
• still	**adj** not moving
• ambush	**n** hiding in order to attack by surprise
• predator	**n** an animal that lives by killing and eating other animals
• prey	**n** animals hunted or killed by another animal for food

Practice 3 🔊 04_U1_P3.mp3

A Listen to part of a conversation in a school office. Pay attention to the main situation and answer the question.

Q. What is the conversation mainly about?

    Ⓐ The difficulty of being a first year student
    Ⓑ The problems with studying for a course
    Ⓒ How to make course selections
    Ⓓ Looking for places on campus

B Listen again and fill in the blanks.

> **M:** Hi, there.
>
> **W:** Oh, hi. I am having some _____ with my course _____. Can you help me?
>
> **M:** Sure. What seems to be the problem?
>
> **W:** Um ... everything, actually. You see, I'm a first year student and I _____ _____ understand the course names. I mean, the codes and numbers....
>
> **M:** Well, I understand. Many first year students have _____ with it.
>
> **W:** I'm glad to hear that. _____ _____ I know I'm not the only one.
>
> **M:** So tell me what _____ _____ courses you want to take. Then I'll help you find them in the course _____.
>
> **W:** Thanks.

- **selection**   **n** the act of making choices; a carefully chosen collection of things

Part II

 05_U1_P4.mp3

A Listen to part of a lecture in a physiology class. Then answer the following questions.

Q1. What is the main topic of this lecture?

Ⓐ The origin of the word 'borborygmi'
Ⓑ Several signs of an unhealthy stomach
Ⓒ The normal process of stomach noise
Ⓓ Problems caused by a hungry stomach

Q2. What is 'borborygmi'?

Ⓐ A hungry stomach
Ⓑ A type of brain signal
Ⓒ A growling stomach sound
Ⓓ Digestive juice

Q3. According to the lecture, which of the following cause stomach noise?

Click on 2 answers.

Ⓐ The size of the stomach
Ⓑ The contractions of digestive organs
Ⓒ The type of food in the stomach
Ⓓ The mixture of gas and digestive juice

• physiology	**n**	the biological study of living organisms
• growl	**v**	to make a deep sound
• digestive	**adj**	relating to the process of taking and converting food in the body
• tighten	**v**	to make or become tight
• intestine	**n**	the parts of the long tube-like organs extending from the stomach to the anus, that helps to digest food and absorb nutrients and water and that carries waste matter to be discharged
• contraction	**n**	the shortening and thickening of a working muscle or muscle fiber
• squeeze	**v**	to press together from the opposite sides

B Listen again and find the correct words from below to complete the summary.

> Growling 1._____ of the Stomach: borborygmi

How it happens: hungry ➔ think about 2._____
➔ send signals to 3._____ organs
➔ 4._____ of the stomach and intestines
➔ digestive juices mix with 5._____
➔ squeeze through small 6._____
➔ make noises

Normal and 7._____

- gas
- food
- noise
- healthy
- digestive
- contraction
- opening

Practice 5 🔊 06_U1_P5.mp3

A **Listen to part of a lecture in a history class. Then answer the following questions.**

Q1. What does the professor mainly discuss?

  Ⓐ How wasps and caterpillars react to each other
  Ⓑ How a type of plant reacts to a pest
  Ⓒ Why caterpillars fear wasps
  Ⓓ Why there are many wasps in a cornfield

Q2. Why does the professor mention wild chimpanzees?

  Ⓐ To review what the class discussed last time
  Ⓑ To introduce a new type of animal reaction
  Ⓒ To compare chimpanzees with caterpillars
  Ⓓ To give an example of an enemy of plants

Q3. How do caterpillars harm the corn plant?

  Ⓐ By chewing the leaves
  Ⓑ By attracting wasps to ruin the plant
  Ⓒ By melting it with toxic saliva
  Ⓓ By making it smell strong

• enemy	**n** something that harms
• be invaded	be disturbed or violated
• pest	**n** a plant or an animal harmful to human or other organisms
• caterpillar	**n** the wormlike larva of a butterfly or moth
• harm	**v** to hurt or damage
• chew	**v** to crush or grind with the teeth
• saliva	**n** a watery mixture discharged into the mouth
• emit	**v** to send out or eject
• wasp	**n** a winged insect related to bees and ants
• hatch	**v** to produce from eggs
• offspring	**n** the young of a person, animal, or plant
• feed on	to take as food

B Listen again and find the correct words from below to complete the summary.

How corn plants 1._____ to caterpillars

Caterpillars:
2._____ the corn leaves

The corn plant:
3._____ a chemical

Wasps:
- 4._____ the chemical and fly over
- lay eggs on the caterpillars
- offspring 5._____ the caterpillars

Caterpillars die
➡ The corn plant is
6._____

- emit
- smell
- protected
- chew
- feed on
- react

Practice 6   06_U1_P6.mp3

A Listen to part of a conversation between a student and a teacher. Then answer the following questions.

Q1. What is the conversation mainly about?

ⓐ Getting more time to work on the assignment
ⓑ Attending a family funeral
ⓒ Missing a few days of classes
ⓓ Going to Boston to work on the assignment

Q2. Why does the student ask for more time to work on the assignment?

ⓐ She wants to add a few more pages.
ⓑ She has to go to a funeral this weekend.
ⓒ She has a problem understanding the assignment.
ⓓ She thinks the deadline is unreasonable.

• be due	expected or scheduled to arrive
• pass away	to die
• exception	**n** a case where a rule does not apply
• reasonable	**adj** not excessive or extreme; rational

B Listen again and find the correct words from below to complete the summary.

W:

Assignment due on
1. _____

Go to Boston for grandmother's
2. _____

Want a few more days for the assignment

M:

Will make an 3. _____ to accept late assignments

Can give 4. _____ more days

Finish it by 5. _____

· two   · Monday   · Wednesday   · exception   · funeral

Test 1

Q1. What is the lecture mainly about?

    Ⓐ How spiders build their webs

    Ⓑ Why spider webs are so useful

    Ⓒ How spiders use trees for hunting

    Ⓓ The special organs and glands of spiders

Q2. Why does the speaker mention spider webs?

    Ⓐ It is the most unknown fact about spiders.

    Ⓑ It is the easiest fact to understand about spiders.

    Ⓒ It is the strangest thing about spiders.

    Ⓓ It is spiders' most famous feature.

Q3. What are spinnerets?

    Ⓐ Another name for spider webs

    Ⓑ Special organs for making a web

    Ⓒ A type of spider that builds a web in a tree

    Ⓓ Recycled spider webs

Q4. According to the speaker, what helps spider silk reach the tree branches?

Ⓐ Breezes
Ⓑ Insects
Ⓒ Its strength
Ⓓ Old webs

Q5. Why does the speaker think that spiders are smart?

Ⓐ They can build webs on high branches.
Ⓑ They recycle old webs to make new ones.
Ⓒ They can hunt insects with their webs.
Ⓓ They use threads to walk between trees.

- strung   v (past tense and past participle of string) to stretch out or extend
- spin   v to make thread by drawing out and twisting fibers
- gland   n an organ that produces a substance for use elsewhere in the body
- thread   n a thin cord of natural or manufactured material
- breeze   n a gentle wind
- recycle   v to process in order to regain materials for use

Natural Science

Test 2

Q1. What is the main topic of the discussion?
- Ⓐ The different respiratory systems of insects
- Ⓑ The possible sizes of prehistoric insects
- Ⓒ The earth's atmosphere 300 million years ago
- Ⓓ The basic features of dragonflies

Q2. What does the professor say about prehistoric dragonflies?
- Ⓐ They were much smaller in size.
- Ⓑ They had different features.
- Ⓒ They had different respiratory systems.
- Ⓓ They were much bigger in size.

Q3. How was the earth 300 million years ago different from today?
- Ⓐ It had more oxygen in the atmosphere.
- Ⓑ It had less oxygen in the atmosphere.
- Ⓒ It had only few types of insects.
- Ⓓ It had a greater number of insects.

Q4. Which of the following is true about an insect's respiratory system?

    Ⓐ It has many lungs.

    Ⓑ It has many air-filled tubes.

    Ⓒ It doesn't require oxygen to breathe.

    Ⓓ Its lungs are connected by tubes.

Q5. According to the professor, what determines the size of an insect?

    Ⓐ The number of air-filled tubes

    Ⓑ The amount of oxygen in the air

    Ⓒ The size of its wingspan

    Ⓓ The amount of its muscle mass

• prehistoric	**adj** of the era before recorded history
• wingspan	**n** the distance between the tips of a pair of wings as of a bird or an airplane
• respiratory system	a system or organs used in breathing
• air-filled	containing air
• atmosphere	**n** the whole mass of air surrounding the earth
• tissue	**n** a mass or layer of cells that form the basic structure material of a plant or an animal
• muscle	**n** a body tissue made of long cells that can contract and produce motion
• mass	**n** a large amount of a solid substance, a liquid, or a gas

Natural Science

Test 3

10_U1_T3.mp3

Q1. What is the conversation mainly about?

Ⓐ Having difficulty with a Spanish course
Ⓑ Changing the student number
Ⓒ Making a course change
Ⓓ New guidelines for taking courses

Q2. Why can't the man take the morning session of Spanish 101?

Ⓐ He has to work in the morning.
Ⓑ It is not being offered this year.
Ⓒ He is taking another course.
Ⓓ It is already closed.

Q3. Why does the woman mention the deadline?

Ⓐ To explain why he can't take the Spanish course
Ⓑ To remind the man about another important date
Ⓒ To make sure that the man's change is final
Ⓓ To encourage the man to choose another course

- session   ⓝ a period of time for a specific activity or class
- be closed   not be able to add to the list or enter for an activity
- deadline   ⓝ a time limit

Listening Helper 🔊 11_U1_LH.mp3

A. Listen to each sentence and fill in the blank with the correct word(s) you hear. 🎧

1. Scientists make _____ maps of species to solve the mystery of evolution.
2. Signals from the brain _____ the stomach and intestines with more contractions.
3. The corn plant _____ certain chemicals to protect itself from its pests.
4. Even the slightest _____ in the air can carry the thread from tree to tree.
5. You can see spider webs _____ high in the branches between two trees.
6. It's perfectly normal for your stomach to make _____ sounds when you're hungry.
7. Insects breathe through a network of _____ tubes.
8. John is not in class today because his grandmother _____ _____.

B. First, listen to each sentence to complete the blank with the correct word(s). 🎧
Then choose the word that has the same meaning as the word from the recording.

1. Flowers completed most of their _____ process in only 30 million years.
   Ⓐ developmental   Ⓑ growing   Ⓒ revolutionary

2. Cats can _____ the movement of their prey very well.
   Ⓐ affect   Ⓑ see   Ⓒ control

3. Ambush predators usually stay _____ before they attack.
   Ⓐ hard   Ⓑ motionless   Ⓒ on top

4. Gas and the digestive juices make noises as they _____ through the intestine.
   Ⓐ press   Ⓑ open   Ⓒ scream

5. When the wasp eggs hatch, these offspring _____ the caterpillars.
   Ⓐ feel   Ⓑ provide for   Ⓒ eat

6. There was more room in an insect's body for other _____ to grow.
   Ⓐ paper   Ⓑ cells   Ⓒ bones

7. Professor Jenson never allows _____ regarding assignments.
   Ⓐ special cases   Ⓑ exercise   Ⓒ extra

8. I can't register for the Spanish morning session because it _____ already.
   Ⓐ is not far away   Ⓑ is full   Ⓒ is tight

Natural Science

UNIT 02

Academic Lectures: History
Conversations

•• Key Expressions

The speaker may use certain expressions or words as a signal to mention important details in the lecture.

• You should remember that…	• especially
• This is actually interesting because…	• absolutely
• It's important to keep in mind…	• consider
• One thing I want to mention here is that…	• make sure
• The best way is to…	• necessary
• It is true that…	• fact

•• Target iBT TOEFL Questions

Academic lectures

What does the speaker say about…?
Which of the following is true about…?
According to the lecture, what is…?

Conversations

What is the conversation mainly about…?
What does the woman suggest to the student?

Practices

Warm Up 🔊 12_U2_WU.mp3

First, circle one of the words inside the bracket to complete each sentence with your own choice. Then listen to the recording to check the correct answer.

1. The Southern states in 19th century America were more (rural / urbanized) than the North.

2. The Great Fire of London happened in the (Victorian / Medieval) period.

3. Old Canada Road was developed between the province of Quebec in Canada and the state of (Maine / New York) in the United States.

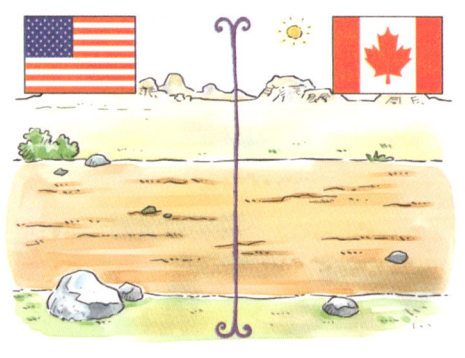

4. In the 1850s, many people went to California looking for (gold / land).

Part I

Practice 1

A Listen to part of a lecture in a history class. Pay attention to specific details and answer the question.

Q. Which of the following correctly describes the South in the 19th century?

　Click on 2 answers.

　Ⓐ People tried to build more factories.
　Ⓑ Cotton farming became quite important.
　Ⓒ Many slaves were educated to read and write.
　Ⓓ Tradition and honor were valued greatly.

B Listen again and fill in the blanks.

> **Prof(W):** After America _____ from British rule, the difference between the South and the North became more _____. By the beginning of the 19th century, Southern states depended largely on cotton farming, using slaves as their _____. However, in the North, a lot of factories were built to produce manufactured goods. The people in the South would _____ how many slaves they _____. On the other hand, the Northerners would be _____ the new machinery in their factories. There were also social and cultural differences between the two regions. Many people in the South didn't have _____ and therefore, could not read and write. The historians say that this was because the South was more _____ compared to the North, which was more _____. They also _____ different things. The people in the South valued _____ and _____, but the Northern people _____ change and progress.

• labor force	a group of people who provide the services usually for pay
• manufacture	**v** to make a raw material into a finished product with the use of machines
• brag about	to speak proudly of; to show off
• machinery	**n** machines or machine parts considered as a group
• rural	**adj** characteristic of the country ↔ urban

History •• 31

Practice 2  14_U2_P2.mp3

A Listen to part of a lecture about the Great Fire of London. Pay attention to specific details and answer the question.

Q. Why did the fire spread so quickly?

Ⓐ Because there was no wind in the air
Ⓑ Because houses were built very close together
Ⓒ Because there weren't many people to put out the fire
Ⓓ Because the fire fighters were out of the city at that time

B Listen again and fill in the blanks.

Prof(M): The Great Fire of London in 1666 was one of the biggest _____ that happened in _____ London. It first started in a baker's shop owned by Thomas Farynor, who was the baker for King Charles II. As you know, the houses in London at that time were mainly _____ _____ and built very close together. So the fire quickly _____ from house to house. There was also a strong wind that helped the fire to _____. Unfortunately, the City of London did not have _____ _____ at that time. People just tried to _____ the fire with buckets of water from hand pumps, but the fire was too _____ to stop. After four days, the fire finally _____. By then, it had destroyed almost 80% of the city, including 13,000 houses. However, only six people were _____ _____ after the fire. Can you believe it? Although it was a great disaster for the city, most people were able to _____ safely from it.

• disaster	**n**	something that happens suddenly and causes much suffering or damage
• medieval	**adj**	of the Middle Ages in history
• baker	**n**	a person who bakes bread for living
• put out		to make things on fire stop burning; extinguish
• bucket	**n**	a round container for carrying liquid

Practice 3 🔊 15_U3_P3.mp3

A Listen to part of a conversation between two people. Pay attention to specific details and answer the question.

Q. Why is the woman coming back on Monday?

Ⓐ She had the wrong information about the due date.
Ⓑ The registrar's office will open on Monday.
Ⓒ The finance office is closed for the day.
Ⓓ She forgot to bring her registration form.

B Listen again and fill in the blanks.

W: Can you tell me where I should go to _____?

M: You should go to the finance office. It's _____ the registrar's office.

W: Okay, thanks.

M: Oh, but wait, I think it's _____ for the day.

W: Really? It's _____ 5 o'clock yet!

M: Well, they close early on Fridays.

W: I see. I guess I drove _____ here for nothing.

M: I'm sorry to hear that.

W: Well, it's my _____. I _____ checked before I came.

M: You still have a few days before the _____.

W: I know. I'll just come back on Monday.

- **tuition** ⓝ money paid for learning, especially at a formal institution
- **registrar's office** a school office that handles student registration

Part II

Practice 4  16_U2_P4.mp3

A Listen to part of a lecture in a history class. Then answer the following questions.

Q1. What is the lecture mainly about?

Ⓐ The development of railways between Maine and Quebec

Ⓑ Major market places in Quebec in 1817

Ⓒ An old, rediscovered trail between Maine and Quebec

Ⓓ The experience of Canadian immigrants

Q2. What caused the Canadians to immigrate to Maine?

Ⓐ The completion of a major railway

Ⓑ The bad economy in Quebec

Ⓒ The long history between Maine and Quebec

Ⓓ A better market for crops and livestock

Q3. What was the main reason that Old Canada Road came to be lost?

Ⓐ Major building construction

Ⓑ The development of another trail

Ⓒ The movement of people to Maine

Ⓓ The completion of a major railway

• trail	**n** a rough path across open country or through forests
• region	**n** a large area of land with its own characteristics
• crop	**n** plants such as wheat and potatoes that are grown in large quantities for food
• livestock	**n** animals that are kept on a farm
• economy	**n** the system under which the money, industry, and trade of a country or region are organized
• immigration	**n** the coming of people into a country in order to live and settle there

B Listen again and find the correct words from below to complete the summary.

An old 1._____ between Quebec & Maine: Old Canada Road

At first: movement from Maine to Quebec for 2._____

Later: Quebec's bad 3._____ ➔ immigrated to Maine for 4._____

The completion of a 5._____ : fewer people used it

Forgotten and lost

Recent 6._____

- rediscovery
- trail
- railway
- trade
- economy
- jobs

Practice 5   17_U2_P5.mp3

A Listen to part of a lecture in an American history class. Then answer the following questions.

Q1. What did Levi Strauss do before he produced blue jeans?

   Ⓐ He was a miner.
   Ⓑ He was a tent maker.
   Ⓒ He was a canvas retailer.
   Ⓓ He was a tailor.

Q2. Put the following events related to the history of blue jeans into correct order.

| 1. |
| 2. |
| 3. |
| 4. |

   Ⓐ Strauss noticed the pants the miners were wearing.
   Ⓑ Miners came to California during the Gold Rush.
   Ⓒ Denim was used to make pants.
   Ⓓ Strauss stitched canvas material to sell as pants.

Q3. According to the speaker, which of the following is an interesting outcome of the California Gold Rush?

   Ⓐ Canvas tents
   Ⓑ Gold miners
   Ⓒ Blue jeans
   Ⓓ Salesmen

• outcome	**n**	result; effect
• miner	**n**	one whose work or business is to get minerals from the earth
• canvas	**n**	a heavy woven fabric (usually of cotton or hemp) used for tents and sails
• coarse	**adj**	rough, not fine in texture
• be torn		to be ripped; to be pulled apart into pieces
• stitch	**v**	to do needlework
• retailer	**n**	one who sells products directly to the customer
• dirt	**n**	a filth or soil (as mud or dust)
• stain	**n**	a discolored or soiled spot

B Listen again and find the correct words from below to complete the summary.

An 1._____ of the California Gold Rush

Gold miners: hard work, 2._____ in a canvas tent
Levi Strauss: a canvas 3._____

| Strauss 4._____ miners' pants | Sold pants made of canvas : 5._____ | Used 6._____ to make pants : hide 7._____ | Became blue jeans Popular for 8._____ work |

- denim
- noticed
- dirt
- outcome
- slept
- outdoor
- salesman
- strong

History •• 37

A Listen to a conversation between a student and a staff member at a school office. Then answer the following questions.

Q1. What does the woman need to do first after the conversation?
- Ⓐ Bring a photo
- Ⓑ Get her student ID
- Ⓒ Make a new course schedule
- Ⓓ Line up to talk to her advisor

Q2. What will the advisor do for the woman?
- Ⓐ Take her to the student affairs office
- Ⓑ Help her get a student ID
- Ⓒ Help her schedule courses
- Ⓓ Register her for special courses

• advisor   **n** an educator who advises students in academic and personal matters

B Listen again and find the correct words from below to complete the summary.

M:

Should get 2._____ first

Go to the 3._____ office

Take 4._____ there

After getting the ID, meet the 5._____
→ will help with the course schedule

W:

Make 1._____

Can get it right now

· advisor   · student affairs   · ID   · picture   · course schedule

History •• 39

Test 1 🔊 19_U2_T1.mp3

Q1. What is the main topic of the discussion?
- Ⓐ The beginning of human civilization
- Ⓑ The advantages of farming
- Ⓒ How to domesticate animals
- Ⓓ The importance of trade in human culture

Q2. When did human civilization begin?
- Ⓐ When people began domesticating animals
- Ⓑ When people began building houses
- Ⓒ When people started exchanging products
- Ⓓ When people started farming

Q3. Which of the following are mentioned as important changes after people started farming?
Click on 2 answers.
- Ⓐ People started exchanging their skills.
- Ⓑ People began to wander around to look for food.
- Ⓒ People began keeping animals as livestock.
- Ⓓ People started sharing their food.

Q4. How were dogs useful to humans?

Click on 2 answers.

Ⓐ For hunting
Ⓑ For guarding livestock
Ⓒ For getting meat and skin
Ⓓ For building houses

Q5. What happened after people became skilled at farming?

Ⓐ They struggled to get more food.
Ⓑ They developed other skills and activities.
Ⓒ They built bigger houses to keep their food.
Ⓓ They planted certain types of grasses to get crops.

• nomad	n	a person or group of people with no fixed home who move from place to place
• wander	v	to move about without definite destination
• domesticate	v	to train or adapt an animal or a plant to live in a human environment
• property	n	something owned; a possession
• specialize	v	to concentrate on a particular activity or product
• struggle	v	to make a great effort to overcome someone or something

Test 2

🔊 20_U2_T2.mp3

Q1. What does the speaker mainly discuss?

Ⓐ Thomas Jefferson as the third American President
Ⓑ The influence of the transcontinental railroad
Ⓒ The life of American farmers in the 19th century
Ⓓ Specialized crops during the 19th century

Q2. What did Thomas Jefferson believe in regarding farmers?

Ⓐ They should live independent lives.
Ⓑ They should borrow money from the banks.
Ⓒ They should use less expensive machinery.
Ⓓ They should worry about national economy.

Q3. Why did the farmers begin specializing in corn and wheat?

Ⓐ They were easier to grow.
Ⓑ They were more profitable.
Ⓒ They could be sold overseas.
Ⓓ They were sold by banks.

Q4. How did the life of farmers change at the end of the 19th century?

> Click on 2 answers.

Ⓐ They no longer had to rely on good weather.

Ⓑ They could make a lot of money selling crops.

Ⓒ They were not free from commercial activities.

Ⓓ They had to travel a great distance to work on their crops.

Q5. Which of the following are mentioned as the things farmers had to worry about? Put a check mark in the correct box.

	Mentioned	Not mentioned
Ⓐ Railroad prices		
Ⓑ The national economy		
Ⓒ Trading with neighbors		
Ⓓ Getting bank loans		

- be free from — not worry about
- commercial — **adj** relating to the buying and selling of goods, designed mainly for profit
- lack — **v** to be without or have very little of
- drastic — **adj** extreme; taking effect rapidly
- profitable — **adj** producing an advantageous gain or return
- transport — **v** to carry from one place to another
- transcontinental — **adj** crossing a continent
- overseas — **adj** beyond or across the sea; outside of one's country
- loan — **n** money lent at interest
- shipping — **n** the act or business of transporting goods

Test 3

Q1. Why does the student come to the admissions office?
Ⓐ To find out whether he got admitted by the school
Ⓑ To apply for a job at the admissions office
Ⓒ To get some information on applying for the school
Ⓓ To download some information from the Internet

Q2. Why couldn't the student download the application form from the website?
Ⓐ The website was out of order.
Ⓑ He could not log in to the website.
Ⓒ The form was not ready yet.
Ⓓ He entered the wrong website.

Q3. What does the woman say about the reference letters?
Ⓐ The students should bring them to the office.
Ⓑ The students should not read them.
Ⓒ They should be mailed by next week.
Ⓓ They are not required for admission.

- reference ⓝ a person who is in a position to recommend another; a statement about a person's qualifications
- transcript ⓝ an official copy of a student's educational record

Listening Helper 🔊 22_U2_LH.mp3

A. Listen to each sentence and fill in the blank with the correct word(s) you hear. 🎧

1. A lot of factories were built in the North to produce _____ goods.
2. The people in the South valued tradition and _____ more than change and progress.
3. The Great Fire of London was one of the biggest _____ in Medieval London.
4. Students need to pay their _____ at the finance office.
5. Quebec was a major market for crops, _____, and fish in the early 19th century.
6. Levi Strauss _____ some canvas and sold it as pants.
7. With _____ changes in agriculture, certain crops became more expensive than others.
8. _____ can usually help students with their course schedules.

B. First, listen to each sentence to complete the blank with the correct word(s). 🎧
Then choose the word that has the same meaning as the word from the recording.

1. There was an old _____ between Quebec and Maine that almost disappeared.
   Ⓐ path   Ⓑ tail   Ⓒ woods

2. The people in the South would _____ how many slaves they owned.
   Ⓐ concentrate   Ⓑ show off   Ⓒ discuss

3. Blue jeans were one of the _____ of the California Gold Rush.
   Ⓐ results   Ⓑ outside   Ⓒ causes

4. The pants that the miners wore couldn't last long because of their _____ work.
   Ⓐ course   Ⓑ complicated   Ⓒ rough

5. Before the beginning of agriculture, people _____ looking for food.
   Ⓐ moved from one place to the other   Ⓑ be confused about   Ⓒ ask questions on

6. Some animals were domesticated and became people's _____.
   Ⓐ profits   Ⓑ businesses   Ⓒ possessions

7. When people _____ something, they just traded items with their neighbors.
   Ⓐ were without   Ⓑ loved   Ⓒ closed

8. Mr. Davis agreed to write a _____ letter for my college application.
   Ⓐ dictionary   Ⓑ recommendation   Ⓒ information

History •• 45

UNIT 03

Academic Lectures: Applied Science
Conversations

•• Key Expressions

The speaker may use certain expressions as a signal for the organization of certain information in the lecture.

- One example of this is...
- Let me give you some examples...
- Similarly...
- On the other hand...
- As I said before...

- The reason I mention this is...
- To prove this, the researchers...
- This shows how...
- Therefore, ...
- So, as a conclusion...

•• Target iBT TOEFL Questions

Academic lectures

Why does the speaker mention...?
Why does the speaker say that...?
What does the speaker intend to show by mentioning...?
Why does the speaker say that...?

Conversations

Why does the student tell the staff about...?

Practices

Warm Up 🔊 23_U3_WU.mp3

First, circle one of the words inside the bracket to complete each sentence with your own choice. Then listen to the recording to check the correct answer.

1. Barnacle glue is made of natural (protein / calcium) from shellfish called barnacles.

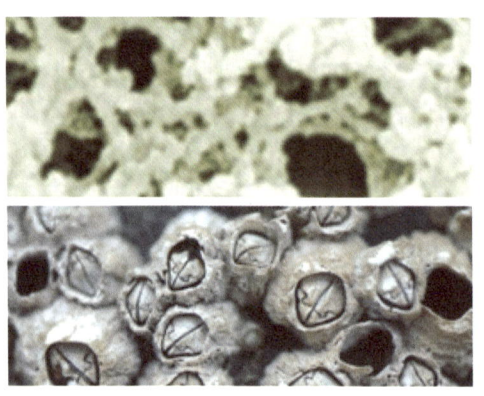

2. The structure of spider webs might give new ideas for designing (furniture / buildings).

3. NASA has been working on sending (humans / water) to Mars as a part of the Mars Project.

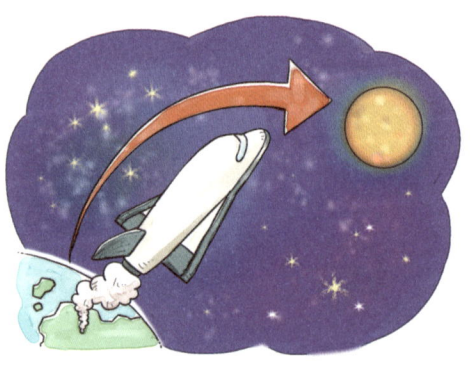

4. Satellites can measure the important (population / climate) changes of our earth.

Part I

Practice 1 🔊 24_U3_P1.mp3

A Listen to part of a talk given in a biochemistry class. Pay attention to how the talk is organized and answer the question.

Q. How does the speaker organize the lecture?

Ⓐ By describing how useful barnacle glue is
Ⓑ By explaining why barnacles stick to rocks or boats
Ⓒ By comparing artificial glue with natural glue
Ⓓ By explaining how to get glue from shellfish

B Listen again and fill in the blanks.

> **Prof(M):** Today, I'd like to talk about a type of glue called "barnacle glue." Barnacle glue is one of the _____ glues you can find in _____. It comes from shellfish called barnacles, which _____ themselves to rocks or the _____ of boats. Because barnacle glue is made of a natural protein, it is considered not _____ like _____ glues. And it is so strong that less than one-inch thickness of the glue can _____ _____ _____ 7,000 pounds. Hard to believe, isn't it? So it makes sense that many biomedical scientists are greatly _____ _____ barnacle glue. According to these scientists, barnacle glue can be used to _____ broken bones or used in dentistry. Research into this material is _____, and it aims to discover even more _____ benefits of barnacle glue.

• shellfish	**n**	an aquatic animal that has a shell
• stick	**v**	to attach with an adhesive material such as glue or tape
• artificial	**adj**	made by humans; not natural or genuine
• dentistry	**n**	the science concerned with the treatment of diseases of the teeth and gums

Applied Science •• 49

Practice 2 🔊 25 _U3_P2.mp3

A Listen to part of a lecture in an engineering class. Pay attention to how the speaker organizes the lecture and answer the question.

Q. Why does the speaker mention a cushion?

Ⓐ To describe the size of an average spider web
Ⓑ To explain where spiders build their webs
Ⓒ To explain how a spider web absorbs shock
Ⓓ To describe how delicate spider webs are

B Listen again and fill in the blanks.

Prof(W): Have you ever seen a spider _____ its prey using a web? Isn't it _____ how such a delicate structure can _____ a powerful tool for a spider? I mean, think about it. Many insects that _____ in a web are often quite big and heavy. It's like capturing an _____ in a fishnet. So what makes a spider web so strong? Well, scientists say that what makes a web so strong is how it is _____. The threads are _____ together in a way to _____ and spread the tension _____ the web. That's why the web is not destroyed when an insect _____ it. Also, the threads are _____ resistant and _____ the shock of the impact like a cushion. So it's no wonder why many experts suggest that the structure of spider webs might lead to _____ for designing buildings.

• capture	**v**	to take something by force
• delicate	**adj**	easily broken or damaged
• fishnet	**n**	a mesh fabric used to catch fish
• resistant	**adj**	unaffected by; proof against
• absorb	**v**	to take in; soak up

Practice 3

A Listen to part of a conversation between two people in a housing office. Then answer the following questions.

Q. How does the man help the student?

    Ⓐ By explaining why she has to apply for student housing
    Ⓑ By giving her more time to bring the application
    Ⓒ By providing the information she needs
    Ⓓ By filling out the application form for her

B Listen again and fill in the blanks.

W: Hi. I'd like to _____ for student housing.

M: Are you currently _____ this university?

W: No, but I will be coming here next year.

M: Oh, I see.

W: So I'd like to find out if I can _____ _____ the student housing program.

M: Well, you'll have to apply first to find out.

W: What kind of _____ do you have?

M: This brochure will tell you which types of housing are _____.

W: Okay. When is the _____ for the application?

M: It's not until July. But the rooms _____ _____ quite quickly.

W: I see. I guess _____ _____ hurry then.

M: That'll be my _____.

• brochure   ⓝ a magazine or thin book with pictures that gives information
• fill up   to become full

Part II

 Practice 4 🔊 27 _U3_P4.mp3

Ⓐ Listen to a talk given by a lab assistant. Then answer the following questions.

Q1. What is the talk mainly about?
- Ⓐ Where to get the workbook
- Ⓑ How to use the workbook
- Ⓒ How to choose a lab assistant
- Ⓓ How to start today's experiment

Q2. What does the speaker say about the experiments in the workbook?
- Ⓐ Students are required to do all of them.
- Ⓑ They are difficult material for students to do.
- Ⓒ Only some of them will be covered in the semester.
- Ⓓ They are chosen by the lab assistants.

Q3. What is the speaker willing to do for the students?
- Ⓐ Help them choose some material from the workbook
- Ⓑ Decide which experiments to do today
- Ⓒ Order the workbooks from the bookstore
- Ⓓ Help them finish the lab experiment

• lab	ⓝ	a place equipped for making scientific experiments and tests
• assistant	ⓝ	a helper
• workbook	ⓝ	a booklet that has problems and exercises for a student to work on
• material	ⓝ	ideas or information that is to be made into something with an effort
• cover	ⓥ	to deal with
• experiment	ⓝ	a procedure carried out under specific conditions in order to discover something
• hesitate	ⓥ	to stop or pause because of uncertainty; to be unwilling

B Listen again and find the correct words from below to complete the summary.

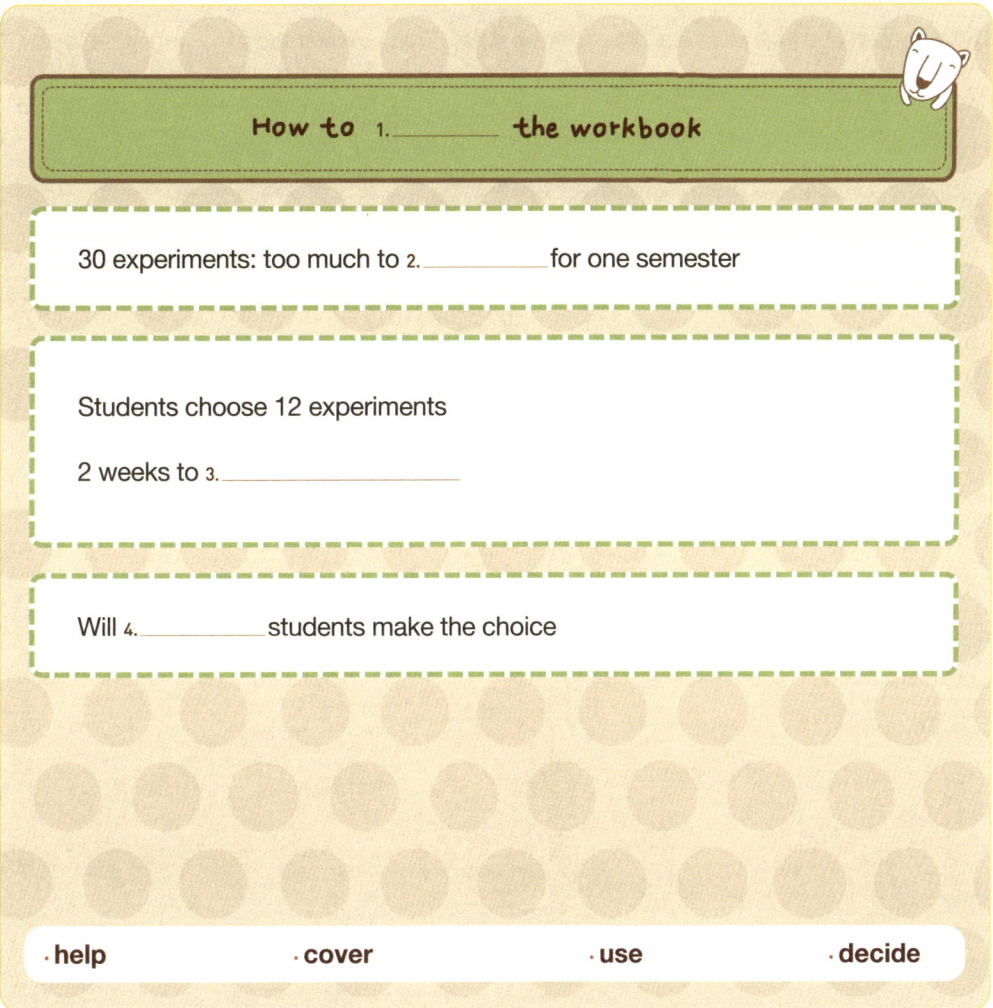

How to 1._____ the workbook

30 experiments: too much to 2._____ for one semester

Students choose 12 experiments

2 weeks to 3._____

Will 4._____ students make the choice

· help   · cover   · use   · decide

Practice 5 28_U3_P5.mp3

A Listen to part of a lecture in a space science class. Then answer the following questions.

Q1. What is the speaker's main point?

Ⓐ NASA's satellites are causing a disaster on the earth.
Ⓑ New satellites are more expensive than sending humans to Mars.
Ⓒ Studying the earth's changes is also important work for NASA.
Ⓓ Sending a satellite to Mars is easier than sending a human.

Q2. According to the professor, what is happening to NASA's satellites?

Ⓐ They are being destroyed by spaceships to Mars.
Ⓑ Many of them will stop working soon.
Ⓒ They can measure climate change on Mars.
Ⓓ They are becoming less expensive to replace.

Q3. Why are NASA's satellites important?

Ⓐ To understand the earth's changes
Ⓑ To successfully send humans to Mars
Ⓒ To save money on the Mars Project
Ⓓ To study the climate of Mars

• dilemma	**n**	a situation in which one has to make a difficult choice
• resource	**n**	something that can be used for support or help
• satellite	**n**	an object intended to orbit the earth
• life cycle		the lifetime of a thing or an organism
• measurement	**n**	a result usually expressed in numbers that are taken by measuring something
• budget	**n**	the amount of money available for spending

B Listen again and find the correct words from below to complete the summary.

NASA'S 1._____

Studying the earth's environment **Vs.** Sending 2._____ to Mars

Fewer 4._____ available

More serious problem
- need new 5._____
- need to understand the earth's 6._____
- if not, could bring a 7._____

Too much 3._____ on the Mars project

Use a lot of resources

- disaster
- humans
- resources
- dilemma
- changes
- focus
- satellites

Practice 6 🔊 29_U3_P6.mp3

A Listen to part of a conversation between two people on campus. Then answer the following questions.

Q1. What is the man's problem?

  Ⓐ He doesn't like his roommate.

  Ⓑ He can't afford to rent an apartment.

  Ⓒ He doesn't want to live in the woman's building.

  Ⓓ He hasn't found a place to live next year.

Q2. What does the woman say about her place?

  Ⓐ The rent is too expensive.

  Ⓑ It's not near the campus.

  Ⓒ Its location is very convenient.

  Ⓓ Her roommate doesn't like it.

• dormitory	**n** a building for housing a number of persons at a school
• afford	**v** to manage; to have enough money or means for something
• outrageous	**adj** very offensive; being beyond all reason
• vacancy	**n** an empty or unoccupied space
• superintendent	**n** a person whose job is to look after a large building such as an apartment

B Listen again and find the correct words from below to complete the summary.

W:	M:

Had the same difficulty finding an apartment
 	
Happy but too 4._____ from the campus
Might be a 5._____
Will speak to the 6._____
	Not coming back to the 1._____
	Can't afford 15% 2._____ increase
	Looking for an apartment with a friend
	  - not easy
	
	Woman's place
	  - rent is 3._____
	  - near the subway

- superintendent
- dormitory
- far
- reasonable
- vacancy
- fee

Test 1

Q1. What is the discussion mainly about?

    Ⓐ Why people use the Internet

    Ⓑ Different types of Internet addiction

    Ⓒ The various benefits of using the Internet

    Ⓓ How to use information from the Internet

Q2. Which of the following is mentioned as a type of Internet addiction?

Check the appropriate boxes.

	Mentioned	Not mentioned
Ⓐ Cyber relationships		
Ⓑ Net gaming		
Ⓒ Organizing information		
Ⓓ Online research		
Ⓔ Information overload		

Q3. According to the professor, why do people experience information overload?

    Ⓐ It is fun and convenient.

    Ⓑ People are naturally curious about things.

    Ⓒ People need to look at a lot of data.

    Ⓓ It is a fast way to meet people.

Q4. What does the student say about pictures and video clips?

Ⓐ They are not available on the Internet at this time.
Ⓑ He doesn't really look at them after downloading them.
Ⓒ He needs to collect them for his school.
Ⓓ It takes too much time to collect them.

Q5. What does the professor say about being too involved in a cyber relationship?

Ⓐ People may get closer to their real life friends.
Ⓑ People could lose their real life friends.
Ⓒ It is very common for young people.
Ⓓ It causes people to fail at work or school.

• be addicted	to be dependent; be hooked on
• addiction	**n** having a very strong desire or need for something
• cyberspace	**n** the online world of computer networks
• gambling	**n** playing a game for money or property
• put aside	to keep something to be dealt with at a later time
• overload	**n** having more than one can handle
• curious	**adj** interested in something and wanting to know more about it

Test 2 🔊 31_U3_T2.mp3

Q1. What is the main topic of the lecture?
- Ⓐ The types of organisms on the earth
- Ⓑ Photosynthesis in plants
- Ⓒ The importance of heat and light
- Ⓓ Energy from the sun

Q2. What does the speaker say about the amount of energy absorbed by the earth?
- Ⓐ It is only a small percent of the total energy from the sun.
- Ⓑ It increases when the temperature of the earth increases.
- Ⓒ It is not large enough to change the world.
- Ⓓ It changes from time to time.

Q3. How does heat affect the earth?
- Ⓐ It creates carbon dioxide and water.
- Ⓑ It provides the necessary temperatures for life.
- Ⓒ It blocks ultraviolet radiation.
- Ⓓ It increases the amount of visible light on the earth.

Q4. Why does the speaker mention colors and shapes?

　Ⓐ To explain how light is used by humans

　Ⓑ To describes the influence of heat energy

　Ⓒ To mention how heat energy changes

　Ⓓ To show how light affects green plants

Q5. What is created during photosynthesis?

　Ⓐ Carbon dioxide

　Ⓑ Water

　Ⓒ Sunlight

　Ⓓ Carbohydrates

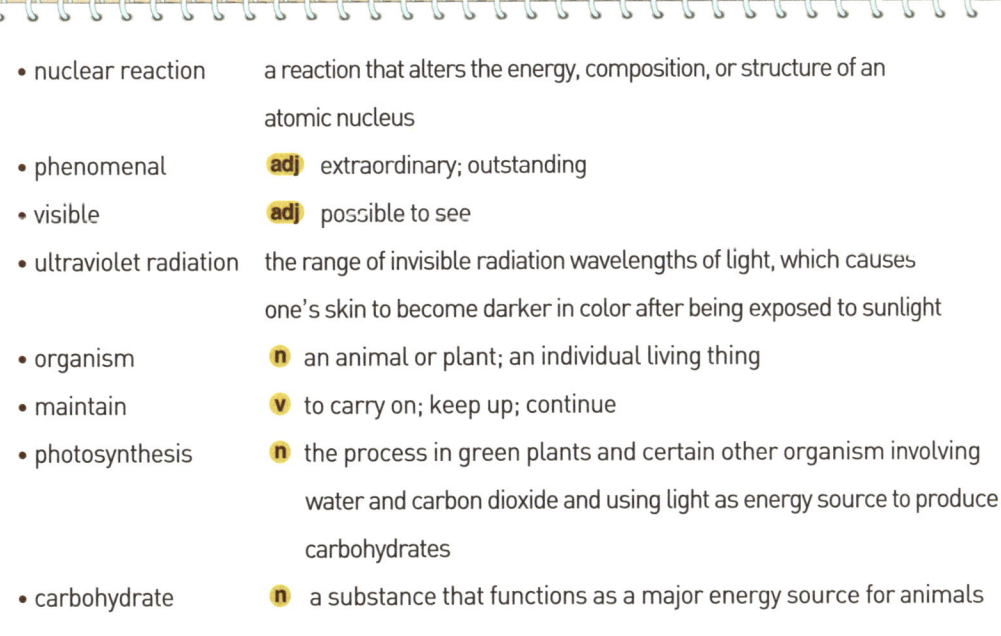

• nuclear reaction		a reaction that alters the energy, composition, or structure of an atomic nucleus
• phenomenal	**adj**	extraordinary; outstanding
• visible	**adj**	possible to see
• ultraviolet radiation		the range of invisible radiation wavelengths of light, which causes one's skin to become darker in color after being exposed to sunlight
• organism	**n**	an animal or plant; an individual living thing
• maintain	**v**	to carry on; keep up; continue
• photosynthesis	**n**	the process in green plants and certain other organism involving water and carbon dioxide and using light as energy source to produce carbohydrates
• carbohydrate	**n**	a substance that functions as a major energy source for animals

Test 3 🔊 32_U3_T3.mp3

Q1. What is the conversation about?
- Ⓐ A new cafeteria in student housing
- Ⓑ Some changes in the student meal plans
- Ⓒ Some problems with cafeteria food
- Ⓓ The importance of eating every meal

Q2. Why does the student say this:
- Ⓐ He apologizes for his mistake.
- Ⓑ He is unhappy with the woman's attitude.
- Ⓒ He wants the woman to throw something at him.
- Ⓓ He didn't hear what the woman just said.

Q3. What does the woman say about the meal plan?
- Ⓐ Many students complain about it.
- Ⓑ She doesn't understand it very well.
- Ⓒ It will benefit the students.
- Ⓓ It changes every week.

Q4. What does the student decide to do?
- Ⓐ Eat his breakfast from now on
- Ⓑ Pay for all three meals
- Ⓒ Think more about his options
- Ⓓ Get 10 meals per week

- meal plan — a regular provision of meals that has been paid in advance
- resident — **n** one who lives in a particular place
- complicated — **adj** difficult to understand or deal with

Listening Helper 🔊 33_U3_LH.mp3

A. Listen to each sentence and fill in the blank with the correct word(s) you hear. 🎧

1. Barnacle glue is not harmful like _____ glues.
2. The threads of a spider web are very strong and air _____.
3. Students shouldn't _____ to ask questions to the lab assistant.
4. Many satellites need to be replaced but the _____ is limited.
5. Many people are _____ to playing games on the Internet.
6. The effect of solar energy on the earth is _____.
7. People are _____ about things in nature.
8. Thomas cannot _____ to pay for his dormitory next year.

B. First, listen to each sentence to complete the blank with the correct word(s). 🎧
Then choose the word that has the same meaning as the word from the recording.

1. Barnacles _____ themselves to rocks or the bottom of boats.
   Ⓐ point   Ⓑ attach   Ⓒ extend

2. The threads of a spider web are connected in a way to balance and spread _____.
   Ⓐ nervousness   Ⓑ pressure   Ⓒ worry

3. Many insects that _____ in a spider web are often quite big and heavy.
   Ⓐ results   Ⓑ cover   Ⓒ cut

4. The rooms at the dormitory _____ quite early.
   Ⓐ wake up   Ⓑ clean up   Ⓒ become full

5. There is not enough time to _____ everything in the workbook.
   Ⓐ deal with   Ⓑ spread   Ⓒ wrap

6. The article gives you a general idea about NASA's _____ these days.
   Ⓐ decision   Ⓑ difficult choice   Ⓒ project

7. Jessie will find out if there is a _____ in her building.
   Ⓐ empty spot   Ⓑ vacation   Ⓒ job

8. All _____ are supposed to buy a meal plan separately.
   Ⓐ people living here   Ⓑ school buildings   Ⓒ student doctors

Applied Science •• 63

UNIT 04

Academic Lectures: Education and Language
Conversations

•• Key Expressions

The speaker may use certain expressions as a signal for implied or indirect meanings in the lecture.

- Although...
- Not only... but also...
- It won't be difficult to believe...
- I can't stress enough how important this is...
- It is no surprise to find that...

•• Target iBT TOEFL Questions

Academic lectures

What does the speaker imply about...?
What can be inferred about...?
What does the speaker mean when he says...?

Conversations

What does the student mean when she says...?
What does the professor imply about...?
What can be inferred about the student from the conversation?

Practices

Warm Up   34_U4_WU.mp3

First, circle one of the words inside the bracket to complete each sentence with your own choice. Then listen to the recording to check the correct answer.

1. Emily Dickinson is a famous American poet who wrote over (700 / 1700) poems.

2. The first English (dictionary / textbook) was written by Robert Cawdrey in 1604.

3. The *Review* was the very first magazine and it was published by a (prisoner / pilot).

4. Exaggeration is one of the many ways to write a (creative / realistic) poem.

Part I

Practice 1

A **Listen to part of a lecture in a literature class. Pay attention to implied meanings and answer the question.**

Q. What does the speaker imply about Emily Dickinson's poems?
   Ⓐ They became famous after she died.
   Ⓑ Many of them were written by her sister and friends.
   Ⓒ It is unclear how they got published.
   Ⓓ They are very unusual and mysterious.

B **Listen again and fill in the blanks.**

Prof(M): Emily Dickinson is one of the most famous _____ in America. Although she wrote over 1700 poems, only ten of them were published in her _____. We know of her work only because her sister and two friends published it after _____. She is known for being an _____ person at that time. Some people even say that she was a _____ person. She never got married and had a very _____ life. It is said that she _____ even left her house. After her death, people found forty volumes of small notebooks _____ her poems. Emily Dickinson _____ those notebooks herself and called them 'fascicles.' Most of Emily Dickinson's poems we know nowadays are from these fascicles.

- **mysterious** adj strange and not known
- **bind** v to hold together by tying a rope, tape, or other material around something

Education and Language 67

Practice 2

Ⓐ Listen to a talk given in a linguistics class. Pay attention to implied meanings and answer the question.

Q. What does the speaker imply about 'A Table Alphabeticall'?

Ⓐ It was written by many scholars.
Ⓑ It is probably the first English dictionary.
Ⓒ It was developed by the University of Toronto.
Ⓓ It is also the first dictionary in the world.

Ⓑ Listen again and fill in the blanks.

Prof(W): Most languages that are spoken in our _____ _____ have dictionaries. Now, do you ever _____ who wrote the first dictionary? Well, I _____ tell you who wrote the very first dictionary in the _____ world. However, we can certainly _____ who wrote the first English dictionary. The name you should remember for our question is Robert Cawdrey. In 1604, Robert Cawdrey wrote a _____ _____ called 'A Table Alphabeticall.' Most _____ of modern English generally _____ that 'A Table Alphabeticall' is in fact the first English dictionary _____ _____. Unfortunately, not much is known about _____ _____ and how he came to write it. However, there is an _____ copy of the text of 'A Table Alphabeticall' at the University of Toronto. You might want to _____ _____ _____ on the Internet if you are interested.

• reference	ⓝ something that people look up to find information or facts about a subject
• scholar	ⓝ a person who studies an academic subject and knows a lot about it

Practice 3 🔊 37 _U4_P3.mp3

Ⓐ Listen to part of a conversation between two people. Pay attention to implied meanings and answer the question.

Q. What does the woman imply about the work-study program?

Ⓐ It is not difficult to get into.
Ⓑ There are different kinds of jobs.
Ⓒ Students will be working only for a few weeks.
Ⓓ Students will start working next week.

Ⓑ Listen again and fill in the blanks.

M: Excuse me. I'm here to _____ _____ the work-study program.

W: Okay. Did you bring the application form?

M: Yes, here it is. Um, do you know when the _____ process begins?

W: Well, we'll contact you next week if you are _____ _____ the program.

M: _____ I start working then?

W: Um, no. The hiring committee will _____ you first. Then they will match you with the _____ _____ job on campus.

M: That makes sense.

W: So it'll take _____ _____ a few weeks before you actually start working.

M: I see.

• work-study program	an academic program for students to gain work experience and make money while continuing their studies
• be qualified	to have the necessary elements in order to work or pass a particular program
• appropriate	**adj** suitable or acceptable for a particular situation

Education and Language

Part II

 **Practice 4** 🔊 38_U4_P4.mp3

Ⓐ Listen to part of a lecture in a journalism class. Then answer the following questions.

Q1. What is the lecture mainly about?

    Ⓐ The history of early magazines

    Ⓑ The life of Daniel Defoe as a politician

    Ⓒ The difference between newspapers and magazines

    Ⓓ The government policies of 18th century England

Q2. What does the speaker say about the novel *Robinson Crusoe*?

    Ⓐ It was criticized by the king.

    Ⓑ It was first published on the *Review*.

    Ⓒ It was written in prison.

    Ⓓ It was written by the publisher of the *Review*.

Q3. What does the speaker imply about 18th century England?

    Ⓐ A lot of magazines were published during that time.

    Ⓑ People were not allowed to criticize the king.

    Ⓒ People were arrested for reading newspapers.

    Ⓓ Magazines were more popular than newspapers.

• journal	**n**	a magazine that reports on things of special interest to a particular group
• domestic	**adj**	national; internal; relating to one's own country
• policy	**n**	a course of action by a government or business chosen in order to guide people in making decisions
• ring a bell		to bring to memory; to be remembered
• publicly	**adj**	in a public manner; openly
• prison	**n**	a place where criminals are locked up
• content	**n**	the subject matter of a written work such as a book or magazine; material
• analysis	**n**	an explanation of the nature and meaning of something

B Listen again and find the correct words from below to complete the summary.

The 1._____ of magazines

The Review (1704)
- the 2._____ magazine
- looked like 3._____
- focused on domestic 4._____ and government policies

Daniel Defoe
- wrote *Robinson Crusoe*
- 5._____ of the *Review*
- the first issue from 6._____ ➔ more 7._____ than the newspapers

The Tattler (1709)
- covered more 8._____ of things

- publisher
- prison
- political
- issues
- variety
- newspapers
- first
- beginning

Practice 5   39 _U4_P5.mp3

Ⓐ Listen to part of a lecture in a writing class. Then answer the following questions.

Q1. What is the main topic of the lecture?

　Ⓐ Eating spicy food

　Ⓑ Several poems about food

　Ⓒ Using exaggeration to write a poem

　Ⓓ The importance of imagination in eating food

Q2. What does the speaker imply about exaggeration in poems?

　Ⓐ It is always necessary.

　Ⓑ It can be unrealistic.

　Ⓒ It is used only for eating food.

　Ⓓ It is the easiest way to write a poem.

Q3. Why does the speaker mention a volcanic eruption?

　Ⓐ To describe how it feels to eat hot peppers

　Ⓑ To give other topics for a poem

　Ⓒ To describe an exciting experience

　Ⓓ To give an example of a realistic poem

• poem	n	a piece of writing in which the words are chosen and carefully arranged for their beauty and sound
• poetry	n	poems regarded as forming a division of literature
• exaggeration	n	enlargement of a fact or statement beyond what is actual or true; an overstatement
• thunder	n	a loud sound that follows a flash of lightning
• imaginative	adj	creative; having a lively imagination
• volcanic eruption		an explosion of a volcano throwing out a lot of hot melted rock, called lava, as well as ash and steam

B Listen again and find the correct words from below to complete the summary.

One way of writing a poem: 1._____

Claiming something to be 2._____

Fun way to write 3._____ poetry

Ex. eating spicy food
- eating hot peppers
➔ 4._____
➔ a volcanic eruption

Writing poem: doesn't have to be 5._____

- fire
- greater
- exaggeration
- imaginative
- realistic

Practice 6 40 _U4_P6.mp3

Ⓐ Listen to part of a conversation between a student and a teacher. Then answer the following questions.

Q1. What is the conversation about?

    Ⓐ Why the student did so poorly on her assignment
    Ⓑ How to take great photos for an assignment
    Ⓒ A mistake the student made on her assignment
    Ⓓ How to find correct information on the Internet

Q2. What does the teacher imply about the photos the student used?

    Ⓐ They should not be used at all.
    Ⓑ They are related to the student's assignment.
    Ⓒ They are better than other information she used.
    Ⓓ They were taken by the teacher himself.

• credit	**n**	recognition or approval for an achievement, act, or quality
• facts and figures		information presented as objectively real

B Listen again and find the correct words from below to complete the summary.

W:	M:
	To talk about woman's 1._____
	Great job
	Woman didn't credit the photos
	Should mention where she 2._____ them
Didn't think she had to credit the photos	
Credited only 3._____	
	First time ➜ let it 4._____
	Shouldn't happen again

· facts and figures   · assignment   · pass   · found

Test 1 🔊 41_U4_T1.mp3

Q1. What is the main topic of the lecture?

Ⓐ Common mistakes in child language
Ⓑ The importance of teaching real words
Ⓒ Several stages of child language
Ⓓ The pronunciation of child language

Q2. How old is a child when she begins to use real words?

Ⓐ 6 months old
Ⓑ 1 year old
Ⓒ 2 years old
Ⓓ 3 years old

Q3. Why might a 3-year-old child say "runned" instead of "ran"?

Ⓐ She likes saying words in longer form.
Ⓑ She probably changes all verbs in the same way.
Ⓒ She cannot pronounce the word properly.
Ⓓ She doesn't understand the past tense yet.

Q4. Put the following stages of child language in correct order.

1.	
2.	
3.	
4.	

Ⓐ Say real words like "mama" and "dada"

Ⓑ Start to use past tense forms

Ⓒ Put two words together at a time

Ⓓ Make sounds like "ga-ga-ga-ga-ga"

Q5. What can be said about 2-year-old children?

Ⓐ They know more than 1000 words.

Ⓑ Their pronunciation is not very clear.

Ⓒ They cannot describe what happened in the past.

Ⓓ They do not speak real words.

- gurgle — **v** to express or pronounce with a broken or irregular sound
- babble — **v** to make a meaningless confusion of words or sounds
- distinct — **adj** clearly defined
- progress — **n** development; advancement

Test 2 🔊 42_U4_T2.mp3

Q1. What do the speakers mainly discuss?

Ⓐ Understanding pictures in writing

Ⓑ Ancient Egyptian writing

Ⓒ Two different forms of writing systems

Ⓓ Ancient and modern pictograms

Q2. What can be said about modern-day pictograms?

Ⓐ They are more accurate than ancient ones.

Ⓑ They can be found in public places.

Ⓒ They only represent abstract ideas.

Ⓓ They are more popular than ideograms.

Q3. Which of the following is mentioned in the discussion about ideograms?

Click on 2 answers.

Ⓐ They are not used in modern times.

Ⓑ They were developed by ancient Egyptians.

Ⓒ They are more symbolic and abstract than pictograms.

Ⓓ They do not represent words in any specific language.

Q4. Why does the student talk about his experience at an airport in another country?

　　Ⓐ To explain how he understood signs without knowing the language
　　Ⓑ To explain why he had to learn pictograms and ideograms
　　Ⓒ To describe examples of symbolic writings in another language
　　Ⓓ To describe the difference between pictograms and ideograms

Q5. Which of the following could be represented in pictograms?

　　Ⓐ A movie schedule
　　Ⓑ English poems
　　Ⓒ Different animals in a zoo
　　Ⓓ A textbook on computer programming

• pictogram	**n**	a system of picture writing
• ideogram	**n**	a system of writing to represent a thing or an idea but not a particular word or phrase
• symbolic	**adj**	having the function or meaning of a symbol
• abstract	**adj**	expressing a quality or idea not based on an actual person or thing
• be on the right track		to say or do something correctly in general
• be reserved		to be kept for someone; to be set aside
• disabled	**adj**	handicapped; crippled; weakened

Education and Language

Test 3

🔊 43_U4_T3.mp3

Q1. Why does the student come to see the woman?
- Ⓐ To apply for a job at the bookstore
- Ⓑ To get information about the summer internship
- Ⓒ To learn more about book marketing
- Ⓓ To ask for a recommendation letter

Q2. What can be inferred about the student?
- Ⓐ He doesn't have a lot of work experience.
- Ⓑ He wants to study marketing this summer.
- Ⓒ He used to work for the woman.
- Ⓓ He is certain that he will get the job.

Q3. What does the woman imply when she says this: 🎧
- Ⓐ She will write a good letter about him.
- Ⓑ She can help him do better in his new job.
- Ⓒ She will recommend other jobs for him.
- Ⓓ She is uncertain about what to write in the letter.

- **favor** — n doing something for someone to help or support them
- **intern** — n someone who is being given practical training under supervision
- **recommendation** — n a favorable statement about one's character or qualifications; approval
- **marketing** — n the organization of the sale of a product (e.g. deciding on its price, how it should be advertised, etc.)

Listening Helper 🔊 44_U4_LH.mp3

A. Listen to each sentence and fill in the blank with the correct word(s) you hear. 🎧

1. Most _____ agree that 'A Table Alphabeticall' is the first English dictionary.
2. Daniel Defoe was arrested because he _____ criticized the king.
3. The *Tattler* carried a mixture of news and poetry as well as political _____.
4. _____ means claiming something to be greater than it really is.
5. Ideograms are in more symbolic and _____ forms than pictograms.
6. People shouldn't use online pictures without giving _____.
7. Debby did me a big _____ by giving me her class notes.
8. Many students are _____ for the work-study program.

B. First, listen to each sentence to complete the blank with the correct word(s). 🎧
Then choose the word that has the same meaning as the word from the recording.

1. The *Review* magazine focused on the important _____ issues in England.
   Ⓐ family　　　　　　　　Ⓑ internal　　　　　　　　Ⓒ private

2. Some people say that Emily Dickinson was quite a _____ person.
   Ⓐ strange　　　　　　　Ⓑ incorrect　　　　　　　　Ⓒ complicated

3. The _____ of the *Review* was more political than that of newspapers.
   Ⓐ meaning　　　　　　　Ⓑ size　　　　　　　　　　Ⓒ material

4. There are several ways to write _____ poetry.
   Ⓐ creative　　　　　　　Ⓑ thoughtful　　　　　　　Ⓒ realistic

5. A child's pronunciation may not be _____ at first.
   Ⓐ far away　　　　　　　Ⓑ clear　　　　　　　　　Ⓒ different

6. A wheelchair sign means that that the spot is _____ for disabled people.
   Ⓐ set aside　　　　　　　Ⓑ rebuilt　　　　　　　　Ⓒ hidden

7. The hiring committee will match the student with the _____ job.
   Ⓐ professional　　　　　Ⓑ suitable　　　　　　　　Ⓒ training

8. My professor gave me an _____ letter for getting into an advanced class.
   Ⓐ approval　　　　　　　Ⓑ informal　　　　　　　　Ⓒ instruction

Education and Language

UNIT 05

Academic Lectures: Nature and Society
Conversations

•• Target iBT TOEFL Questions

Academic lectures

What does the speaker mean when he says this?
What is the speaker's purpose when she says this?
Listen again to part of the lecture. Why does the speaker say this?

Conversations

Why does the student say this?
What does the professor mean when she says this?
Listen again to part of the conversation. Why does the speaker say this?

Practices

Warm Up 🔊 45_U5_WU.mp3

First, circle one of the words inside the bracket to complete each sentence with your own choice. Then listen to the recording to check the correct answer.

1. Along with snowfall, low temperatures and a lack of (sunlight / water) are required to form a glacier.

2. Infants are born without any (choice / culture) and, therefore, have no sense of social behavior.

3. Ice Age people faced their homes toward the south to get more (sunlight / air).

4. A jury is a group of people who are supposed to learn about a case in (a trial / an election).

Part I

 46_U5_P1.mp3

A Listen to part of a lecture in an earth science class. Pay attention to the meaning and purpose of special expressions and answer the question.

Q. Why does the speaker say this?

Ⓐ She expects the students to explain it.
Ⓑ She thinks it is unbelievable.
Ⓒ She is upset that it doesn't make sense.
Ⓓ She wants the students to think about it.

B Listen again and fill in the blanks.

Prof(W): Many people think that glaciers are the _____ heavy snowfall. Well, that's _____ true, but there are many places in the world without glaciers, _____ _____ they get a lot of snow. On the other hand, many areas in the Arctic and Antarctic only get small amounts of snow, but they have a lot of glaciers. Now, how can you explain that? So our question for today is, what _____ a glacier? Well, of course, snowfall is _____ for glacial formation, but what's important is that the snow must be _____. This means that the temperature in the area has to be _____ so that the snow doesn't _____. Also, it has to be _____ _____, where the amount of sunlight is limited. Another important condition is that the saved snow doesn't get _____ _____ by wind. So _____ _____ the snowfall and low temperatures, both a lack of sunlight and wind are _____ to form a glacier.

• Arctic   **n** / **adj**   the area of the world around the North Pole
• Antarctic   **n** / **adj**   the area around the South Pole
• shade   **n**   an area where sunlight doesn't reach

Practice 2 47_U5_P2.mp3

A **Listen to part of a lecture in a sociology class. Pay attention to the purpose of special expressions and answer the question.**

Q. What does the speaker mean when he says this:

Ⓐ Students shouldn't ask any questions.
Ⓑ Something is very obvious.
Ⓒ He doesn't have any more questions.
Ⓓ The question can't be answered.

B **Listen again and fill in the blanks.**

Prof(M): As a member of a society, there are certain things we _____ and certain things we _____ do. Of course, we didn't know this when we were infants. No question about that. Infants are _____ _____ any culture and have _____ _____ of social behavior. Their parents, their teachers, and other people instruct them while they are _____ _____. Through these lessons, they _____ culture and become a member of society. Now, do you remember how you _____ to eat at the table or clean your hands? You probably _____ your mother or big brother doing the same thing and learned from them. So children learn to walk, talk, and behave properly _____ _____ other people. They also learn through _____ and punishments. For example, a mother _____ good behavior by smiling at or hugging her baby. On the other hand, if the baby behaves badly, she might punish the baby with a frown or _____ _____ scolding.

• infant	**n**	a child in the earliest period of life
• observe	**v**	to become aware through careful attention
• reward	**n**	something given or received for good and desirable behavior; a prize
• frown	**v**	to wrinkle the forehead to express anger or displeasure
• scolding	**n**	an act of speaking angrily about someone's misbehavior

Practice 3

A Listen to part of a conversation between two people. Pay attention to the main situation and answer the question.

Q. What does the man mean when he says this:

　Ⓐ He didn't know that she was in the student council.
　Ⓑ He read about the student council on the newspaper.
　Ⓒ He thinks her involvement with the student council is interesting.
　Ⓓ He heard some news about the student council.

B Listen again and fill in the blanks.

> **M:** Hey, Diane, what are you doing?
>
> **W:** Oh, hi, Henry. As you _____, I'm making a poster for the book sale on campus.
>
> **M:** Oh, yeah, I heard about it. Isn't it _____ by the student council?
>
> **W:** Yes, it is, and I'm the cultural event _____ for the student council.
>
> **M:** Oh, that's _____ to me. Anyway, _____ are you guys getting the books to sell?
>
> **W:** Well, we get _____ from several publishing companies and the local libraries.
>
> **M:** Hey, can I _____ some of my old books? It's not much, but ....
>
> **W:** Sure. That'll be great. You can _____ to the student council's office by next Friday.

• be hosted by	(an event is) to be organized and provided by
• student council	a group elected by students to serve in a student government
• coordinator	ⓝ one who puts together things that will function with each other
• donation	ⓝ the act of giving without charge; a gift; an offering; a contribution

Part II

A Listen to part of a lecture in an anthropology class. Then answer the following questions.

Q1. What is the main purpose of the discussion?

Ⓐ To study how advanced the Ice Age people were

Ⓑ To explain how people used the sun

Ⓒ To discuss better ways of building houses

Ⓓ To learn about geography during the Ice Age

Q2. What did Ice Age people do that was so smart?

Ⓐ They lived in caves to survive the cold weather.

Ⓑ They used animal skins and bones to build houses.

Ⓒ They faced their shelters toward the south for more sunlight.

Ⓓ They were able to find regions with warmer climates.

Q3. What does the teacher mean when he says this:

Ⓐ The student made a mistake by saying it.

Ⓑ He wanted to say something before the student.

Ⓒ The student said something correct.

Ⓓ He wants to know what the student said.

• anthropology	**n**	the study of people, society, and culture
• cave	**n**	a large hole in the side of a cliff or hill, or one that is under the ground
• shelter	**n**	a small building or covered place made for protection against bad weather or danger
• region	**n**	a large area of land with its own characteristics
• solar heating		a system to provide heat by using sunlight
• cobblestone	**n**	a naturally rounded stone
• insulate	**v**	to protect something from cold or noise by covering it with a thick layer

B Listen again and find the correct words from below to complete the summary.

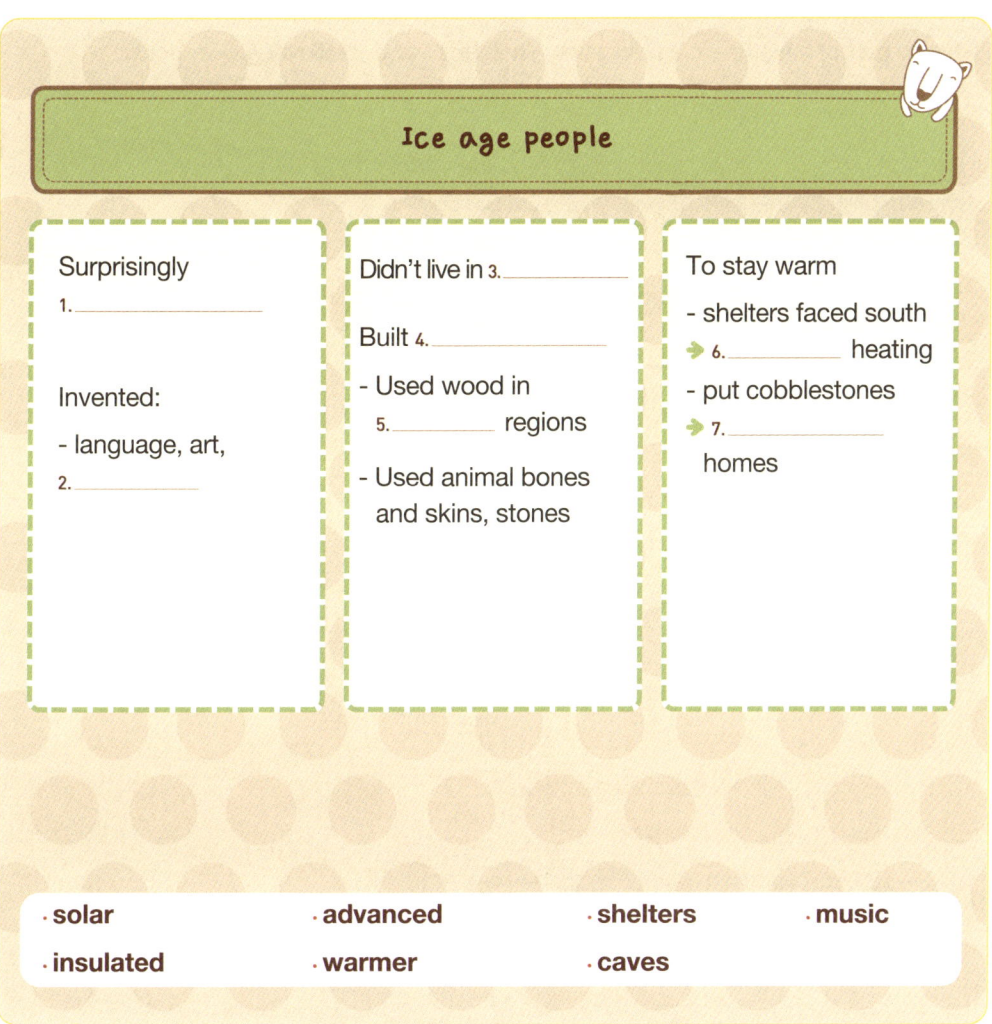

Ice age people

Surprisingly
1. _____

Invented:
- language, art,
2. _____

Didn't live in 3. _____

Built 4. _____
- Used wood in
  5. _____ regions
- Used animal bones and skins, stones

To stay warm
- shelters faced south
  ➜ 6. _____ heating
- put cobblestones
  ➜ 7. _____ homes

- solar
- advanced
- shelters
- music
- insulated
- warmer
- caves

Practice 5 🔊 50 _U5_P5.mp3

Ⓐ Listen to part of a lecture in a law class. Then answer the following questions.

Q1. What is the main purpose of the lecture?

  Ⓐ To compare the modern and the ancient court systems

  Ⓑ To explain the benefits of having juries in law courts

  Ⓒ To describe the court systems of ancient Greece

  Ⓓ To discuss how ancient people were punished for their crimes

Q2. What does the speaker mean when she says this: 🔊

  Ⓐ Not many people feel fortunate about the records.

  Ⓑ The records say a lot about the fortunate people.

  Ⓒ She doesn't really want to talk about the records.

  Ⓓ It is surely great to have the records.

Q3. How did the people in the jury vote in ancient Greek trials?

  Ⓐ By throwing a metal disc into one of the jars

  Ⓑ By placing a jar in front of the person on trial

  Ⓒ By standing next to one of the metal jars

  Ⓓ By picking up a metal disc from different jars

• court	**n**	a place where legal matters are decided by a judge and jury
• jury	**n**	a group of people from the general public who listen to the facts about a crime and decide whether the accused person is guilty or not
• trial	**n**	a formal meeting in a law court to decide whether a person is guilty of a crime
• evidence	**n**	the information (documents, object, or witnesses) used in court to prove something
• disc	**n**	a round and flat shape or object
• vote	**v**	to give one's choice officially at a meeting or in an election
• guilty	**adj**	found to have committed a crime; having done wrong; to blame
• punishment	**n**	a penalty enforced for wrongdoing; discipline

B Listen again and find the correct words from below to complete the summary.

The court of 1._____ Greece

2._____ by jury

Jury: learn the case ➔ decide 3._____ or not
- today: 12 juries
- ancient times: several 4._____

Court process:
1. Jury listens to the 5._____
2. Place a metal disc into a 6._____ to vote
3. Decide guilty or not
4. Court decided the 7._____

- evidence   · punishment   · hundreds   · trial
- jar   · ancient   · guilty

A **Listen to part of a conversation between two people. Then answer the following questions.**

Q1. Why does the woman want to come back?

    Ⓐ The ticket price will go down later.

    Ⓑ She wants to check if her guest can come.

    Ⓒ She didn't bring enough money for the ticket.

    Ⓓ She wants to get a discount ticket somewhere else.

Q2. Why does the woman say this:

    Ⓐ To apologize for what she just said

    Ⓑ To ask the man to repeat what he said

    Ⓒ To express how surprised she is

    Ⓓ To show that she is not interested

• banquet	ⓝ a grand formal dinner celebrating a special occasion or honoring a guest
• be out of town	to be away from where the person lives on a trip or business

B Listen again and find the correct words from below to complete the summary.

W:

To buy 1._____ banquet tickets

Father may come but may be 3._____

Buy one more ticket 4._____

Will 6._____ with father and come back

M:

Single - $50

Double - with a 2._____

No 5._____ for buying separately

$80 for double tickets

- discount
- graduation
- guest
- later
- check
- out of town

Test 1   🔊 52_U5_T1.mp3

Q1. What is the discussion mainly about?

    Ⓐ Natural disasters in the Antarctic continent

    Ⓑ Using the ice shelf to prevent global warming

    Ⓒ Definitions of the greenhouse effect

    Ⓓ One of the signs of global warming

Q2. What do environmental scientists worry about?

    Ⓐ The unusual weather in the Antarctica

    Ⓑ The breaking of the ice shelf in the Antarctica

    Ⓒ The increasing amount of ice in the oceans

    Ⓓ The protection of the oceans from weather changes

Q3. What do ice shelves do for the Antarctic continent?

    Ⓐ Raise the level of the continent

    Ⓑ Cause the greenhouse effect

    Ⓒ Protect its ice from melting

    Ⓓ Bring warmer winds

Q4. What does the professor say is the real problem?

Ⓐ The ocean level could rise due to melted ice.

Ⓑ The Antarctic continent will become colder.

Ⓒ There will be more unusual weather changes.

Ⓓ Global warming reduces ocean water levels.

Q5. Why does the student say this:

Ⓐ To reply to the professor's humor

Ⓑ To express her shock

Ⓒ To ask the professor to be serious

Ⓓ To show how upset she is

• shelf	ⓝ	a flat, usually rectangular structure
• Antarctica	ⓝ	the Antarctic Continent; the Antarctic
• prediction	ⓝ	saying or making a statement about what one thinks will happen; a forecast

Nature and Society

Test 2

Q1. What is the main topic of the discussion?

- Ⓐ Dreams and visions in a native culture
- Ⓑ A special trial for native youth in becoming an adult
- Ⓒ The importance of spiritual guardians in a native culture
- Ⓓ Spiritual changes in becoming an adult

Q2. What is the purpose of a vision quest to Native American tribes?

Click on 2 answers.

- Ⓐ To endure physical and emotional trials
- Ⓑ To learn how to sing animal songs
- Ⓒ To be recognized as a shaman
- Ⓓ To find signs of a guardian spirit

Q3. Which of the following is mentioned as what a boy is supposed to do on a vision quest?

Check the correct box for each statement.

	Mentioned	Not mentioned
Ⓐ Make spiritual songs for the guardian spirit		
Ⓑ Go through loneliness and hunger		
Ⓒ See his guardian spirit in a dream		
Ⓓ Walk through the wilderness with a shaman		
Ⓔ Get spiritual guidance for his life		

Q4. What does the student think about a vision quest at first?

Ⓐ She thinks it is too harsh.

Ⓑ She finds it boring.

Ⓒ She thinks it is useless.

Ⓓ She doesn't think it is real.

Q5. What does the teacher mean when he says this:

Ⓐ He also wants to ask the same question.

Ⓑ He is happy with the student's attitude.

Ⓒ He is willing to answer the question.

Ⓓ He was waiting for the student to say something.

• trial	**n**	a test
• vision	**n**	the experience of seeing something in a dream or spiritual situation
• quest	**n**	the act of searching for something; an adventure; a mission
• loneliness	**n**	the unhappiness felt by someone for not having friends or anyone around
• hunger	**n**	a feeling of weakness or discomfort caused by a lack of food
• harsh	**adj**	with no understanding or sympathy; rough; cruel; unkind
• prayer	**n**	the activity of speaking to God, a god, or another object of worship
• guardian spirit		a spiritual or religious being that watches over or protects
• transition	**n**	the process in which something changes from one state to another
• shaman	**n**	someone who acts as a medium between the human world and the spirit world
• interpret	**v**	to translate orally from one language to another

Nature and Society

Test 3

🔊 54_U5_T3.mp3

Q1. What are the two people talking about?

Ⓐ The benefits of being in the campus choir
Ⓑ Joining the campus debate club
Ⓒ How to win a formal debate
Ⓓ Why the man should speak up in the class

Q2. Why does the teacher think the student should join the debate club?

Ⓐ He makes good arguments in class.
Ⓑ It will benefit his study of history.
Ⓒ He knows a lot about history.
Ⓓ He has a lot of debate experience.

Q3. Listen again to part of the conversation. Then answer the following question. 🎧
What does the teacher mean when she says this: 🎧

Ⓐ She is upset that the student doesn't understand her.
Ⓑ She was talking about a different student.
Ⓒ She has a lot to say to the student.
Ⓓ She is serious about what she said.

• cross one's mind		to be thought of; to occur as a thought
• recruit	v	to supply with new members or employees
• argument	n	a discussion in which people try to express their differences in opinion and try to convince each other they are right
• debater	n	someone who takes part in formal debates

Listening Helper 55_U5_LH.mp3

A. Listen to each sentence and fill in the blank with the correct word(s) you hear.

1. Many areas in the _____ get a small amount of snow but have a lot of glaciers.
2. _____ are born without culture and have no sense of social behavior.
3. Children learn how to behave properly by _____ other people.
4. Kelly is the cultural event _____ for the student council.
5. Prehistoric people didn't actually live in _____ .
6. Some _____ with warmer climates had trees even during the Ice Age.
7. _____ is a group of people who are supposed to learn about a case in a trial.
8. The debate club is trying to _____ new members this year.

B. First, listen to each sentence to complete the blank with the correct word(s). Then choose the word that has the same meaning as the word from the recording.

1. The idea that a glacier is the result of heavy snowfall is _____ true.
   Ⓐ not entirely   Ⓑ completely   Ⓒ separately

2. Little children can learn through _____ and punishments.
   Ⓐ repetition   Ⓑ paybacks   Ⓒ prizes

3. Early humans invented a way to _____ their homes with cobblestones.
   Ⓐ guide   Ⓑ protect   Ⓒ invent

4. After listening to the _____ , the people in the jury made their vote.
   Ⓐ discussion   Ⓑ proof   Ⓒ signal

5. According to scientific _____ , the ocean could rise with the melting of ice.
   Ⓐ forecasts   Ⓑ practices   Ⓒ tests

6. There were several signs of the boy's successful _____ to becoming an adult.
   Ⓐ growth   Ⓑ transport   Ⓒ change

7. The shaman _____ the boy's dream and explained it to him.
   Ⓐ interested   Ⓑ translated   Ⓒ claimed

8. _____ are being accepted for the upcoming book sale.
   Ⓐ contributions   Ⓑ suggestions   Ⓒ volunteers

Nature and Society

UNIT 06

Academic Lectures: Arts and Culture
Conversations

•• Target iBT TOEFL Questions

Academic lectures

What is the speaker's attitude when he says this?
What can be said about the speaker when she says this?
What is the speaker's attitude toward…?
Listen again to part of the lecture. What does the speaker mean when she says this?

Conversations

What is the student's attitude when she says this?
Listen again to part of the conversation. What can be said about the librarian?

Practices

Warm Up 🔊 56_U6_WU.mp3

First, circle one of the words inside the bracket to complete each sentence with your own choice. Then listen to the recording to check the correct answer.

1. Chicago became an important city for (cultural / architectural) studies because of the great fire in 1871.

2. In traditional Native American culture, many songs are considered (gifts from spirits / personal property).

3. In ancient Greece, plays were generally performed in an (outdoor / indoor) theater.

4. People did not express themselves freely during the (Renaissance / Victorian) period.

Part I

Practice 1

A **Listen to part of a lecture in an architecture class. Pay attention to the attitude of the speaker and answer the question.**

Q. What can be said about the speaker's attitude toward Chicago's great fire when he says this:

Ⓐ He is unsure why it's called a great tragedy.
Ⓑ He is certain that it was a terrible disaster.
Ⓒ He doesn't think it happened in Chicago.
Ⓓ He has doubts about what really happened.

B **Listen again and fill in the blanks.**

> **Prof(M):** I'm sure many of you heard about Chicago's great fire in your history class. The fire happened in 1871, and it was so _____ that it destroyed _____ Chicago. Yes, it was without _____ a great tragedy. However, it was probably because of this fire that Chicago became an important city for _____ studies. Do you know why? Well, you see, because the fire destroyed most of the _____ buildings in the city, they had to _____ it in many ways. And, during the 1800s, a great number of new building techniques and materials were _____ in America. So many architects and _____ wanted to try these new _____ to build the most _____ structures at that time. Many of these buildings also became the _____ _____ of skyscrapers in America.

• tragedy	**n** an extremely sad event or situation
• architectural	**adj** relating to the design and construction of buildings
• innovative	**adj** inventive; new; original
• skyscraper	**n** a very tall building in a city

Arts and Culture •• 103

Practice 2 58_U6_P2.mp3

A Listen to part of a lecture about Native American music. Pay attention to the attitude of the speaker and answer the question.

Q. What does the speaker think about Native American music?

Ⓐ She thinks there is too much of it.
Ⓑ She finds it too personal.
Ⓒ She thinks it should be performed more often.
Ⓓ She is fascinated by it.

B Listen again and fill in the blanks.

Prof(W): Music is a very important part of Native American life. It is _____ everyday activities like babysitting _____ special occasions such as funerals. Native Americans use music to _____ the weather, for telling stories, greeting one another, and expressing thanks ... well, _____ every aspect of life. I personally find it so _____ how there is such a great _____ of songs. In a traditional Native American community, songs are so important that everyone has to have their own songs. Many songs are _____ as personal property. Therefore, they can only be _____ by the person who _____ them _____, that is, the composer. If another tribe member wants to sing a song that they did not make, they must _____ it from the composer.

• babysitting	**n**	taking care of a baby or child
• funeral	**n**	a ceremony held when the body of someone who has died is buried or cremated
• aspect	**n**	a way in which something can be viewed; point of view; outlook; part; position
• fascinating	**adj**	interesting; attractive
• composer	**n**	someone who writes music

Practice 3

A **Listen to part of a conversation between two people. Pay attention to the attitude of the speaker and answer the question.**

Q. What does the man mean when he says this:

 Ⓐ He might be able to take the bus.
 Ⓑ He can't take the bus.
 Ⓒ He will take the bus.
 Ⓓ He doesn't want to take the bus.

B **Listen again and fill in the blanks.**

M: Oh, no! It's _____.

W: You didn't bring an umbrella?

M: No, I didn't. And I have to walk _____ _____ to my dormitory.

W: Isn't there a shuttle bus from the library? Why don't you take it?

M: I _____ _____ take the bus, but they stopped the shuttle service last week.

W: Really? Why?

M: I guess not _____ people were using it.

W: That's too bad. Well, I hope the rain will _____ _____ soon.

M: I hope so, too.

• **shuttle**   **n** a vehicle that makes frequent trips between two places
• **let up**   to die down; to become less intense

Part II

Practice 4 60_U6_P4.mp3

A **Listen to part of a discussion in a drama class. Then answer the following questions.**

Q1. What is the discussion mainly about?

    Ⓐ The requirements for becoming an actor

    Ⓑ The characteristics of ancient Greek stage

    Ⓒ The masks and costumes used in ancient plays

    Ⓓ The life of actors in modern theaters

Q2. What is the student's attitude toward the actors of ancient Greece?

    Ⓐ She is amazed by what they did.

    Ⓑ She thinks they were less talented.

    Ⓒ She feels sorry for them.

    Ⓓ She thinks they were not real actors.

Q3. Listen again to part of the discussion. Then answer the question.
What does the professor imply about himself?

    Ⓐ He wanted to be an actor a long time ago.

    Ⓑ He doesn't think he is fast and organized.

    Ⓒ He thinks he is talented enough to be an actor.

    Ⓓ He is trying to be an actor in Greece.

• theater	**n**	a building with a stage on which plays and other performances take place
• feature	**n**	a characteristic
• B.C.E	**abb**	Before the Common Era; Before the Christian Era
• outdoor	**adj**	open-air; outside
• mask	**n**	a covering of the face to hide one's identity
• character	**n**	a role or part in a play; a description of a person's features or qualities
• chorus	**n**	a choir; a group of singers
• costume	**n**	the set of clothes worn by actors in a performance
• organized	**adj**	able to plan and work efficiently

B Listen again and find the correct words from below to complete the summary.

The 1._____ of ancient Greek stage theater

Performed 2._____

Actors used masks

One 3._____ and three actors for all plays

Actors handling many 4._____:

- switched masks and 5._____

- talented, fast, and organized

- costumes
- outdoors
- characters
- chorus
- features

Practice 5   61_U6_P5.mp3

A Listen to a professor talking about colors in an art class.

Q1. What is the main idea of this lecture?

   Ⓐ People dressed better during the Victorian period.
   Ⓑ Colors became important during World War I.
   Ⓒ Red was an important color throughout history.
   Ⓓ Color trends are influenced by the type of society.

Q2. Which of the following is true about the Victorian period?

   Click on 2 answers.

   Ⓐ Many women dressed in bright colors.
   Ⓑ Dark green and beige were popular colors.
   Ⓒ People didn't really show their feelings.
   Ⓓ Dark shades of purple and red were popular.

Q3. What does the speaker mean when he says this:

   Ⓐ There is a clear reason why some colors were popular.
   Ⓑ Most people wanted to wear fashionable colors.
   Ⓒ Some colors made people more fashionable.
   Ⓓ No one knew which colors were fashionable.

• perception	**n**	the recognition of things using one's senses
• differ	**v**	to be unlike each other
• trend	**n**	a change or development toward something new or different
• desire	**v**	to wish for; to want
• be reflected		to be shown; revealed; displayed
• decorate	**v**	to make something more attractive by adding things to it
• interior	**n**	the inside part of something

B Listen again and find the correct words from below to complete the summary.

Different 1._____ of colors

Color trends changed throughout 2._____

19th C. Victorian period

Did not 3._____ freely

Reflected on dresses and home 4._____

5._____ shades of purple, brown, red

First World War

Popular colors: khaki, dark green, beige

➔ 6._____ colors

- dark
- history
- decorations
- express
- perception
- army

Arts and Culture •• **109**

Practice 6   62_U6_P6.mp3

Ⓐ Listen to a conversation between two people on a campus. Then answer the following questions.

Q1. What is the man's attitude toward the woman?

Ⓐ Jealous

Ⓑ Curious

Ⓒ Disappointed

Ⓓ Concerned

Q2. What does the Campus Safety Service do for the woman?

Ⓐ Study with her in the library

Ⓑ Drive her to the library

Ⓒ Walk with her to her dorm at night

Ⓓ Take her to a safer place to study

• worn out	very tired; exhausted
• welfare	ⓝ services provided to help with people's living conditions and problems

B Listen again and find the correct words from below to complete the summary.

M:	W:
	Studying for a 1._____ in the library
	Stay until 11 at night
aLate to 2._____ by herself	
	Call the Campus Safety Service
	- two 3._____ walk together
Big and 4._____ campus	
➔ need the service	
	5._____ better in the library

- **walk** · **study** · **volunteers** · **quiet**
- **test**

Arts and Culture •• 111

Test 1

Q1. What is the main topic of the lecture?
   Ⓐ Different ancient cultures in early North America
   Ⓑ Pottery made by ancient Native American people
   Ⓒ The distinctive features of North American culture
   Ⓓ The life of the Hohokam people in ancient Arizona

Q2. What can be said about the Hohokam people?
   Ⓐ They used special tools to make their pottery.
   Ⓑ They were the only native people to make pottery.
   Ⓒ They were famous for eating and drinking a lot.
   Ⓓ They had special ceremonies for making pottery.

Q3. According to the speaker, what gave the Hohokam pottery distinctive designs?
   Ⓐ Clay
   Ⓑ Tools
   Ⓒ A red color
   Ⓓ Thin sides

Q4. Listen again to part of the lecture. Then answer the question.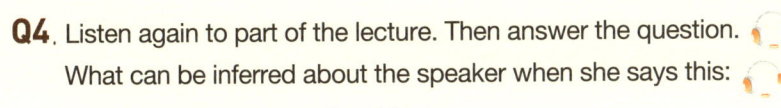
What can be inferred about the speaker when she says this:

Ⓐ She has never seen the objects.

Ⓑ She knows exactly how the objects were used.

Ⓒ She is confused about the objects.

Ⓓ She is somewhat sure about the objects.

Q5. The speaker describes several steps of how Hohokam pottery was created. Put the following steps in correct order.

Ⓐ Create thin sides

Ⓑ Form the pottery vessel

Ⓒ Paint it with a red color

Ⓓ Shape clay into coils

1.	
2.	
3.	
4.	

• pottery	**n**	objects (pots, dishes, etc.) made from clay and then baked in an oven
• C.E.	**abb**	Common Era
• jug	**n**	a large container with a handle used for holding and pouring liquids
• vessel	**n**	a bowl or other container in which liquid is kept
• incense	**n**	a substance that is burned for its sweet smell, often as part of a religious ceremony
• burner	**n**	a device that gets lighted to produce heat or flame
• ritual	**n** / **adj**	a religious service; activities that happen as part of a religious service or tradition
• coil	**n**	a series of connected spirals or rings formed by gathering or winding

Arts and Culture •• 113

Test 2 🔊 64_U6_T2.mp3

Q1. What is the main topic of the lecture?

    Ⓐ The history of musical improvisation

    Ⓑ Famous music played by improvisation

    Ⓒ Methods of musical improvisation

    Ⓓ Recording musical improvisation

Q2. How does the speaker explain the concept of musical improvisation?

    Ⓐ By giving his own performance

    Ⓑ By making the students perform

    Ⓒ By describing how difficult it is

    Ⓓ By providing its history

Q3. Why did prehistoric people have to improvise music?

    Ⓐ They couldn't record music.

    Ⓑ They used it to find food.

    Ⓒ They had to use it for wars.

    Ⓓ They had to prove their musical skills.

Q4. Why does the speaker mention a job interview?

    Ⓐ To explain the importance of an organist

    Ⓑ To explain why organists had to pass a contest

    Ⓒ To explain how people got jobs in the 16th century

    Ⓓ To explain the difficulty of musical improvisation

Q5. Listen again to part of the lecture. Then answer the question.
What is the attitude of the speaker?

    Ⓐ Bored

    Ⓑ Tired

    Ⓒ Excited

    Ⓓ Impatient

- improvisation   **n** something such as music or a speech made without having planned it in advance
- preparation   **n** an arrangement made for a future event or purpose
- on the spot   without preparation; at once
- organist   **n** someone who plays the organ

Test 3 🔊 65_U6_T3.mp3

Q1. Why does the man come to the clinic?

Ⓐ To schedule a medical checkup
Ⓑ To apply for a summer job
Ⓒ To file for medical insurance
Ⓓ To pay for his medical checkup

Q2. Why does the man need a medical statement?

Ⓐ He has to use his insurance service.
Ⓑ He needs it to apply for his insurance.
Ⓒ He wants to check his general health.
Ⓓ His employer asks for it.

Q3. Listen again to part of the conversation. Then answer the question.
What can be said about the man?

Ⓐ He doesn't have his insurance.
Ⓑ He thought he had to pay for his checkup.
Ⓒ He can't afford to pay for his checkup.
Ⓓ He thinks the woman is making a joke.

- medical checkup   an examination of one's physical condition for health purposes
- lifeguard   ⓝ a person who works at a beach or swimming pool and rescues people from drowning
- medical statement   a document issued by a medical doctor or hospital regarding someone's state of health

Listening Helper 🔊 66_U6_LH.mp3

A. Listen to each sentence and fill in the blank with the correct word(s) you hear. 🎧

1. Many architects and builders wanted to try new _____ to build new structures.
2. One of the new buildings became an early model of _____ in America.
3. The song can only be performed by the _____.
4. The actors switched masks and _____ during the play.
5. People's _____ of colors may differ depending on the society they live in.
6. The student council offers a number of student _____ services.
7. Special tools were used to form the pottery _____ from coils of clay.
8. Harry is going to work as a _____ at the community center.

B. First, listen to each sentence to complete the blank with the correct word(s). 🎧
Then choose the word that has the same meaning as the word from the recording.

1. There are many _____ buildings in the city of Chicago.
   Ⓐ instant   Ⓑ inventive   Ⓒ expensive

2. Native Americans use music in just about every _____ of life.
   Ⓐ part   Ⓑ plan   Ⓒ expectation

3. I hope the rain will _____ soon.
   Ⓐ become heavy   Ⓑ ease up   Ⓒ move away

4. There are a few unique _____ of Greek stage theaters.
   Ⓐ foundation   Ⓑ positions   Ⓒ characteristics

5. People's attitudes were _____ by how they decorated their homes.
   Ⓐ pointed   Ⓑ complicated   Ⓒ displayed

6. Incense burners were probably used in _____ ceremonies.
   Ⓐ religious   Ⓑ common   Ⓒ special

7. Ted looks quite _____ these days because of his new job.
   Ⓐ damaged   Ⓑ tired   Ⓒ worried

8. In early times, music was made and played _____.
   Ⓐ at once   Ⓑ here and there   Ⓒ anywhere

Arts and Culture

Actual Test

Lecture Q.1-5 67_AT_1.mp3

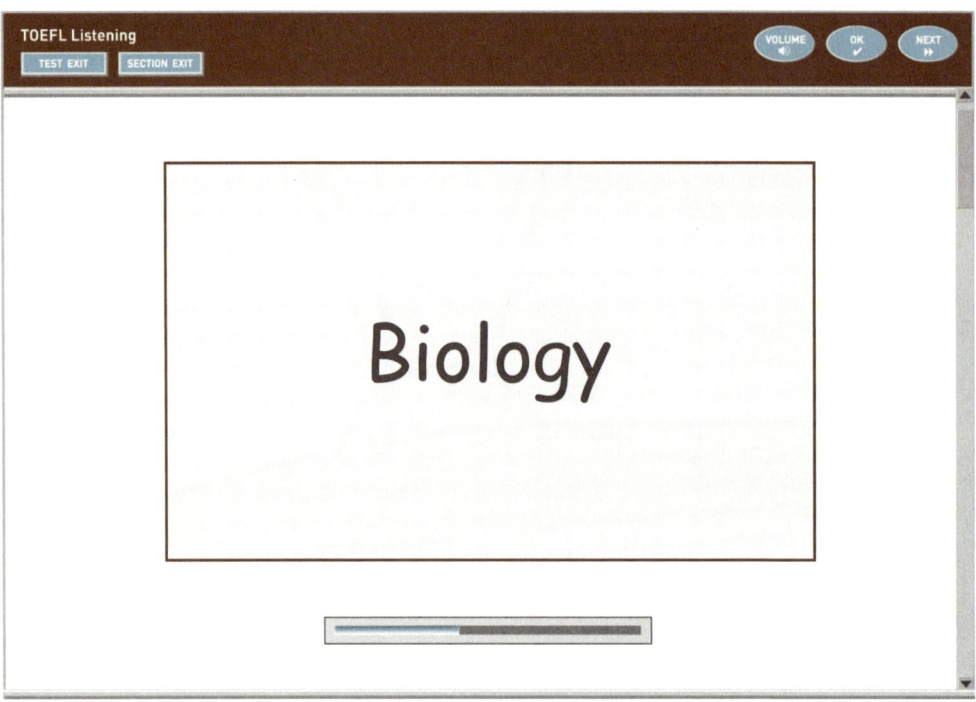

1. What is the lecture mainly about?
    Ⓐ The advantages and disadvantages of camouflage
    Ⓑ The different behavior of animals that use camouflage
    Ⓒ The development of camouflage for colorblind animals
    Ⓓ The factors that influence animal camouflage

2. The speaker mentions how animals have certain colors to blend in with the environment. Match the animal with the correct color. Put a check mark in the correct box.

	Brown	Blue and gray
Ⓐ Dolphins		
Ⓑ Deer		
Ⓒ Sharks		
Ⓓ Squirrels		

3. What is the most important purpose of camouflage?
    Ⓐ To hide from other animals
    Ⓑ To attack predators
    Ⓒ To find a better environment
    Ⓓ To avoid colorblind predators

4. Why does the speaker say this:
    Ⓐ To request that students pay more attention
    Ⓑ To ask if the students have enough space
    Ⓒ To make sure the students have a good understanding
    Ⓓ To check if the students are ready for the lecture

5. According to the lecture, what happens to an animal if its predator is colorblind?
    Ⓐ It will be harder to escape from the predator.
    Ⓑ It can change into many different colors.
    Ⓒ It can still hide by changing its colors.
    Ⓓ It will have to find different ways to hide.

Lecture Q.6 -10 68_AT_2.mp3

6. What is the main topic of the discussion?

　Ⓐ The importance of wildlife for making calendars

　Ⓑ Using arts to advertise companies

　Ⓒ Calendar art with wildlife paintings

　Ⓓ People's attitude toward folk arts

7. How were wildlife calendars used when they first came out?

　Ⓐ To promote the protection of wildlife

　Ⓑ To advertise a certain type of company

　Ⓒ To make money for the wildlife artists

　Ⓓ To change people's attitude toward art

8. What does the professor say about the quality of wildlife calendar arts?

　Ⓐ They were not very artistic.

　Ⓑ They were not real arts.

　Ⓒ They were quite artistic.

　Ⓓ He is not sure about them.

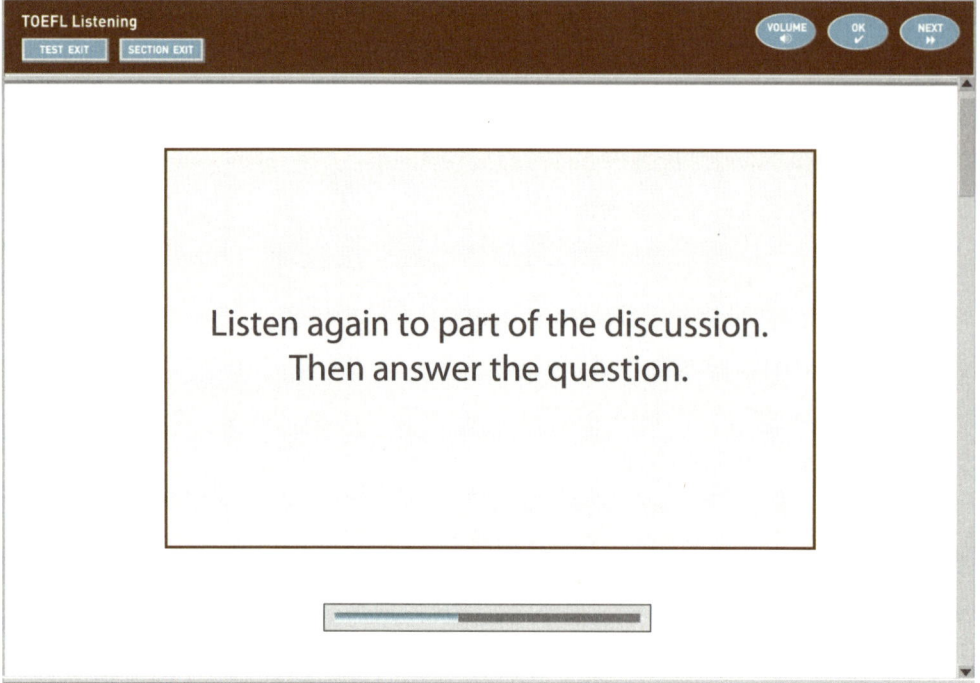

9. What does the professor mean when he says this:

   Ⓐ He doesn't have enough information.
   Ⓑ He somewhat disagrees with the student.
   Ⓒ He doesn't understand the comment.
   Ⓓ He is not interested in the student's opinion.

10. How has wildlife art changed over the years?

    Ⓐ It shows hunting and fishing as more exciting.
    Ⓑ There are more humans in the pictures.
    Ⓒ It is more focused on peaceful nature now.
    Ⓓ Its artistic quality has improved.

Conversation Q.11-13 69_AT_3.mp3

Note

11. What is the student's problem?

    Ⓐ He wants to graduate next semester.

    Ⓑ He cannot take psychology courses.

    Ⓒ He doesn't want to go to summer school.

    Ⓓ He wants to take three summer courses.

12. What does the student ask the woman to do for him?

    Ⓐ Sign a permission form

    Ⓑ Speak to his academic advisor

    Ⓒ Help him concentrate on his studies

    Ⓓ Allow him to graduate on time

13. What is the attitude of the advisor toward the student?

    Ⓐ Surprised

    Ⓑ Concerned

    Ⓒ Disappointed

    Ⓓ Confident

Lecture Q.14-17

14. What is the main purpose of the speaker in this lecture?

    Ⓐ To prepare the students for a writing assignment

    Ⓑ To introduce one of his favorite memoirs

    Ⓒ To compare a memoir and a novel

    Ⓓ To get more information about the students' lives

15. How does the speaker begin the lecture?

    Ⓐ By reading someone's memoir

    Ⓑ By describing the characters of a memoir

    Ⓒ By explaining how to write a memoir

    Ⓓ By giving some examples of a good memoir

16. How is a memoir different from an autobiography?

    `Click on 2 answers.`

    Ⓐ It is written with more emotion.

    Ⓑ It describes one's life in general.

    Ⓒ It may not be completely true.

    Ⓓ It focuses on meaningful moments.

17. What does the speaker say about a good memoir?

    `Click on 2 answers.`

    Ⓐ It needs to be interesting.

    Ⓑ It can be about everyday things.

    Ⓒ It can be exaggerated.

    Ⓓ It should be similar to a novel.

Lecture Q.18-22 71_AT_5.mp3

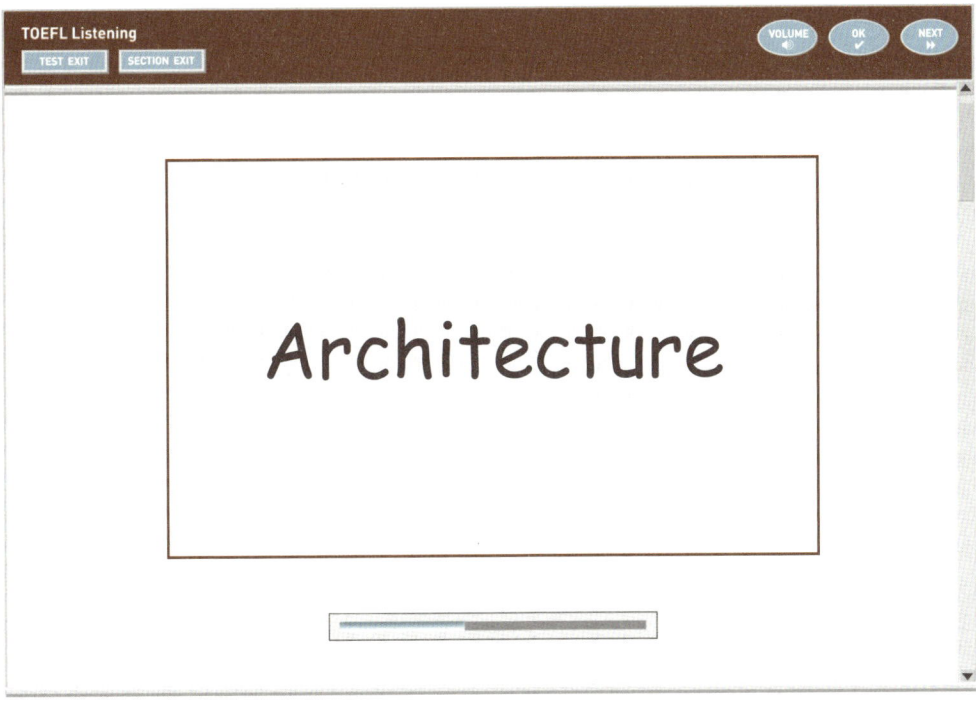

18. What is the main topic of the lecture?

Ⓐ Different ways to build a log house

Ⓑ The advantages of modern log houses

Ⓒ The history of log cabins in America

Ⓓ American presidents and log cabins

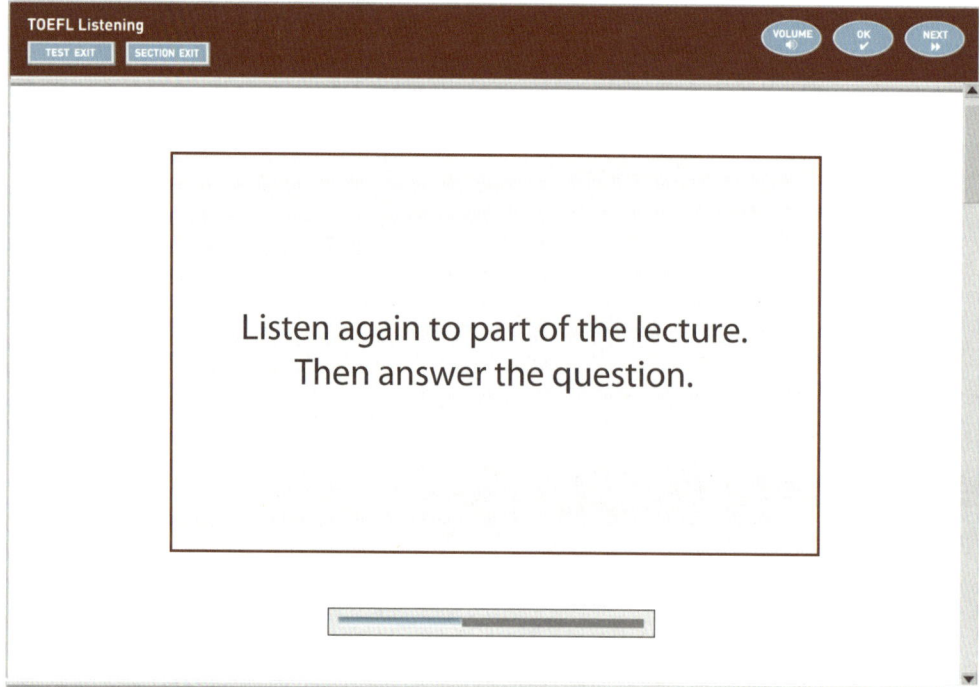

19. What does the speaker mean when he says this:

Ⓐ He wants the students to make a guess.

Ⓑ He is going to say something interesting.

Ⓒ He thinks the students are not interested in the topic.

Ⓓ He is hiding something from the students.

20. What can be inferred about the European immigrants in the Delaware River Valley?

Ⓐ They brought their own logs from their home countries.
Ⓑ They had a difficult time when they were building their homes.
Ⓒ They were familiar with log cabins before coming to America.
Ⓓ They had to plant many trees to get logs.

21. Why were log cabins so popular in the 1800s?

Ⓐ They were cheap and simple to build.
Ⓑ They protected people from many hardships.
Ⓒ They became a symbol of pioneer life.
Ⓓ They were easily built by using a package.

22. Why does the speaker mention Abraham Lincoln?

Ⓐ To show how he used a log cabin to gain popularity
Ⓑ To explain how he built his own log cabin
Ⓒ To describe his life as a pioneer of log cabins
Ⓓ To explain why log cabins became so popular

Conversation Q.23-25 72_AT_6.mp3

Note

23. What is the conversation mainly about?

  Ⓐ The difficulty of studying physics

  Ⓑ How to choose a good tutor

  Ⓒ Working as a physics tutor

  Ⓓ Requesting a tutoring service

24. What can be inferred about the woman?

  Ⓐ She is certain that the tutor will help the student.

  Ⓑ She is confused about the tutor's schedule.

  Ⓒ She is unsure about the quality of the tutor.

  Ⓓ She is unclear why the man needs a tutor.

25. What does the man mean when he says this:

  Ⓐ He has to work on Thursday afternoon.

  Ⓑ He is free on Thursday afternoon.

  Ⓒ He is meeting someone on Thursday.

  Ⓓ He can only come on Thursday afternoon.

Wit&Wisdom iBT TOEFL Series

Intermediate (60~90)

The iBT TOEFL Series

★★
The iBT TOEFL
Reading / Listening / Speaking / Writing

The iBT Grammar Series

★★★
The iBT Grammar
Practice Test

Wit&Wisdom iBT TOEFL Series

Advanced (90~110)

The iBT TOEFL Solution Series

★★★
The iBT TOEFL Solution
Reading / Listening / Speaking / Writing

The iBT TOEFL Master Series

★★★★
The iBT TOEFL Master
Reading / Listening / Speaking / Writing

The iBT TOEFL Actual Test Series

★★★
The iBT TOEFL Actual Test
Vol. 1 / Vol. 2 / Vol. 3